Revelations

Revelations

There's a Light After the Lime

Pastor Mason Betha
with Karen Hunter

POCKET BOOKS
NEW YORK LONDON TORONTO SYDNEY SINGAPORE

POCKET BOOKS, a division of Simon & Schuster, Inc
1230 Avenue of the Americas, New York, NY 10020

All Bible quotations taken from the King James Bible.

ISBN: 0-7434-3418-8

First Pocket Books hardcover printing November 2001

10 9 8 7 6 5 4 3

POCKET and colophon are registered trademarks of
Simon & Schuster, Inc.

For information regarding special discounts for bulk purchases,
please contact Simon & Schuster Special Sales at 1-800-456-6798
or business@simonandschuster.com

Designed by Joseph Rutt

Printed in the U.S.A.

To Jesus. I love Jesus for all He's done for me.

I think my most distinct quality even to this day is my voice. When I was in school people used to say, "He's slow." They would laugh. "Let him read," they would beg the teacher. The teacher would say, "You don't put any emphasis on what you say. Your reading is boring." And then everybody would laugh. Most girls would make jokes at me saying, "spit it out, spit it out." I would say always, "I ain't slow. I'm just calm."

I put time into what I say. I don't just speak. Some people say whatever's on their mind. But I put thought into what I say. Then I became famous for it. Today I don't speak slow when I'm preaching the word of God. And they ain't laughing anymore. . . .

CONTENTS

On April 9, 1999 at approximately 8:05 P.M., Ma$e, noted rapper who sold more than three million copies of his first album Harlem World, *was pronounced dead. He left behind four cars—one Range Rover, a silver BMW, a black Tahoe, a black Mercedes SL convertible, and jewelry worth more than $200,000, a multimillion dollar recording deal with Bad Boy Records, dozens of women from the west coast to the east coast and a few unnamed countries outside the United States, and a host of other fans and groupies. His cause of death: Jesus Christ.*

Elder Gus, the senior statesman of Salvation Deliverance Church on 116th Street in Harlem, was the preacher on this particular Sunday. He stood there in his white robe that hung loose over his body, gripping both sides of the pulpit with a courageous conviction and he said words I will never forget.

"God is about to do a new thing," he said. "I know y'all hear that all the time. But I'm telling you, God is about to do a new thing. He said something to the effect of: God is not waitin' for you Christians. He will go into the gutters, into the crack houses, into entertainment and find men and women who are willing to preach the gospel!"

And he looked up as if he was staring right at me. I was sitting in the balcony with a skull cap on and a hoodie over that. But it was like he picked me out of the crowd. And I'm thinking, "What is he talking about? And what's this got to do with me?"

I had not been to church since Easter or Christmas—you know one of them holidays when people who ain't been to church all year make an appearance. And I had no idea why I went that day. I had spent the night before sexing and drinking. I woke up that morning looking for some weed to smoke when my girl asked me totally out of the blue if I wanted to go to church. Church? My mind was saying, "I don't think so!" But my mouth said, "Yeah." So I put on some jeans that hung off my behind and I threw on a hoodie, finished my joint, and went to church probably smelling like weed.

As I came into the door I walked past an old lady who grabbed my arm and said, "God's gonna bless you today, young man, I see it already."

I was like, "Whatever!" and made my way to the balcony. I didn't want to see anybody and I didn't want anybody seeing me. I got a seat in a corner of the balcony and Elder Gus was doing the altar call.

"By the end of the service God is going to do something that eyes haven't seen, ears haven't heard, or the mind hasn't thought," he said. "Watch it happen today. God's gonna do a new thing. God's gonna do a new thing!"

I'm thinking, "Alright, you said God's gonna do a new thing already! When's he gonna do it?" Never did I think for once that I was a part of the new thing.

Elder Gus kept preaching and by the time he got to the actual altar call, I felt something move inside me. It was like God was saying to me, "Get up out that seat, Mason! You're tired of being Ma$e, tired *of complaining about what comes with the industry, tired of being in the industry. Tired of record labels. Tired of having people around you only because you have money."*

God said, "Are you tired of lying to yourself about being happy? Get up out the seat. Do you want to know what kind of man you are? Get out the seat. Do you want to know how powerful you are without an iced-out chain? Get out of that seat. Does the money make you? Do the cars make you? Stay in that seat. But if you want the answers to the questions you have about your life, get up, Mason. Get up!"

And I did.

—*from* Revelations, Chapter One

He brought me also out of a horrible pit, out of the miry clay, and set my feet upon a rock, and established my goings.

And he hath put a new song in my mouth, even praise unto our God: many shall see it, and fear, and shall trust in the LORD.

—Psalm 40:2-3

———

PART ONE

Old Testament

The Lime

ONE

God's Going to Do a New Thing

Elder Gus, one of the preachers at the Salvation Deliverance Church on 116th Street in Harlem, was leading the altar call on this particular Sunday. He was short and stocky with slicked-back hair. He was one of them hummin'-and-moanin' preachers. He stood at the altar in his white robe, gripping both sides of the pulpit with a conviction that I'd never seen before.

And he spoke these words that I will never forget:

"God is about to do a new thing," he said. "I know y'all hear that all the time. But I'm telling you, God is about to do a new thing. He is not going to wait for you Christians. He will go into the gutters, into the crack houses, into entertainment, and find men and women who are willing to preach the gospel!"

And he looked up as if he was staring right at me. I was sitting in the balcony with a fitted hat on and a hoodie over that.

But it was like he picked me out of the crowd. And I'm thinking, "What is he talking about? And what's this got to do with me?"

I had not been in church since Easter or Christmas—one them holidays when people who ain't been to church all year make their grand appearance. And I had no idea why I went that day. I had spent the night before sexing and drinking. I woke up that morning smoking weed when my girl asked me totally out of the blue if I wanted to go to church. Church?

I don't think so!

But my mouth said, "Yeah." So I put on some jeans that hung off my behind and I threw on a hoodie, finished my joint, and went to church smelling like weed.

As I came to the door, I walked passed an old lady who grabbed my arm and said, "God's gonna bless you today, young man, I see it already."

Whatever . . .

I wanted to be in the front of the church, but I didn't want to see anybody and I didn't want anybody seeing me. So I grabbed a front row seat in the balcony. Elder Gus was doing the altar call.

"By the end of the service God is going to do something that eyes haven't seen, ears haven't heard, or the mind hasn't thought," he said. "Watch it happen today. God's gonna do a new thing. God's gonna do a new thing!"

I'm thinking, All, you said God's gonna do a new thing already! When's he gonna do it?

Elder Gus kept preaching, and by the time he got to the actual altar call, I felt something move inside me. It was like God was saying to me, "Get up out of that seat, Mason! You're tired of being Ma$e, tired of complaining about what comes with the industry, tired of being in the industry. Tired of doing shows. Tired of allowing the radio to pimp you so they would play your music. Tired of the record labels. Tired of having people around you only because you have money."

God said, "Are you tired of lying to yourself about being happy? Get out the seat. Do you want to know what kind of man you really are? Get out the seat. Do you want to know how powerful you are without an iced-out chain? Get out of that seat. Does the money make you? Do the cars make you? If they do, stay in that seat. But if you want the answers to the questions you have about your life, get up, Mason. Get up!"

And I did. Because I really wanted an answer.

I got up, with my fitted hat in my hand and my hoodie. I had on my baggy jeans and my Timberland boots and I walked down the stairs to the sanctuary. My girl was in shock. She couldn't believe how I got up and walked there.

I walked through the sanctuary with my hat balled up in my hand and started down the aisle toward the altar. I could hear people were going crazy as I continued down the aisle. I think a few people even pulled out their cell phones and two-ways and were like, "Yo! Ma$e is at the altar!"

I don't know what came over me. The Holy Ghost just snatched me up and I was at that altar crying. I don't even know why I was crying, I was just crying. And when I finished, Ma$e was gone. God was doing a new thing. Hallelujah!

Another elder asked me what I did for a living. He couldn't understand why the young people in the church were so excited. I said, "I'm a rapper." He said, "No, you used to be a rapper."

"Mister, you might not want to say that," I said.

"God is not a man," he replied. "What God says is what's going to happen even if you don't want it to happen."

He's crazy. That's why I don't come to church.

"God is going to use you in a miraculous way," he said.

Here they go again. Every time I come to church people are trying to tell me how God is going to use me.

But this time *did* feel different. It felt real.

I met Elder Paul Lloyd downstairs. He was in charge of counseling after salvation. Elder Paul continued where Elder Gus left off.

I asked him, "Do I have to give up rap?"

He just said, "God wants you to leave your old life behind and start a new thing."

"Does that mean I have to give up rap?" I asked again.

"God wants you to start a new life," he said.

"I can't gospel-rap or nothing?" I asked.

"It's not for me to tell you yes or no," he said. "But what you're doing now is not of God. I'm going to let God tell you where you need to take it and what you're supposed to do."

I'm supposed to get all this money from Bad Boy. If I quit now, I ain't gonna get this money. So I'm sitting there, stressed out. Bad Boy and I were renegotiating for a couple of million dollars. I was heading to Los Angeles the next week to meet with my manager. I figured I would talk to him about it and he would find a way for me to stay in the game, get that money, and still serve God.

As soon as I got off the plane, in the airport, I bumped into this white man who asked me if I was a preacher. I was like,

"Do I look like a preacher?!" I got tattoos showing and the whole nine. "I ain't no pastor," I said.

I hooked up with my manager, Phil Robinson, who worked for Magic Johnson. As we were getting into the car he asked me if I wanted to go with him to church. I couldn't believe it.

"Nah, man," I said. "Let's go to the movies, to the Magic Johnson Theaters."

I figured a movie would take my mind off my troubles. After the movies my cell phone rings and it was Michelle, this girl I used to go to school with. She told me that in her church they asked each member to pray for a celebrity for a whole year and watch God move. Since she knew me personally she had been praying for me all year.

"I don't know why I'm telling you this, but God told me to tell you to get out while you still can," she said.

These people are scaring me!

I don't know what's going on at this point. I called my mother and she said, "If that's what God is saying to you, you better listen." She told me it was scaring her to hear what I was telling her, especially seeing what had been happening to rappers at that time. Tupac had been killed. Biggie had just been killed.

"Why are you even entertaining this after what you know?" she asked. "What more do you need to happen?"

I went to church later that day with Phil Robinson— Faithful Central in Los Angeles. It's a church where some celebrities go. Bishop Ulmer was preaching. During the altar call, there I was again, up there crying. L.L. Cool J was sitting in the front pew.

When I got to the altar, Bishop Ulmer asked me, "What are you willing to give up for the kingdom?" He was holding the mic to my mouth and I said, "I'm going to give up rap for the kingdom."

It was the first time I had said it out loud. I looked out and my eyes connected with L's and I could tell he was moved. He could see in my face, that me, Mason Betha, the jokester, was dead serious.

The night before I came out to Los Angeles, I was in Trump Plaza Hotel in Manhattan with a young lady doing what used to be one of my favorite hobbies—sex. During that time, I was having sex about four times a day and even when there wasn't a girl around, I would watch pornographic videos.

I had spent all night in the studio working on my second album. I came back to my room on the forty-fifth floor, overlooking Central Park. On top of the world. I went through my electronic organizer and decided to call Melinda. She lived close enough to get there quickly. Melinda was a dark-skinned young lady with a banging body. She was beautiful.

She came over. I smoked my blunt and proceeded to get busy. No kissing, no foreplay. Midway through, this feeling came over me. It was not the usual feeling. I was getting sick to my stomach. It felt like I was having sex with my sister. I just got up and said, "I can't do this no more!"

I walked around the room, with the condom still on, saying, "I can't do this. I can't do this no more." She couldn't understand what was happening. I couldn't even understand what was happening, but I knew I couldn't do it anymore.

I put on my clothes, dropped cab fare on the bed, and left.

I had to get out of there. I walked around outside and ended up in a Barnes and Noble's on Sixty-sixth Street. I bought a *Living Word Bible*. I was walking around with it under my arm. I was trying to read it without anybody seeing me. I sat down at a table in the corner of the store and opened it. "No man can serve God and money. He will love one and hate the other." That's the first scripture I saw.

I closed the Bible and opened it again. "What does it profit a man if he gains the whole world and loses his very soul?"

After I saw that I closed that joint. It was too scary. Every time I opened the Bible it was like God was talking directly to me.

I hooked up with my man Hud. We were sitting in my Jeep and I had my Bible with me.

"Open it up, man," I said. "Just open it up and tell me what you see."

He opened it and the Scripture wasn't clearly speaking to him. He did it again. Nothing. Why when I did it was there a powerful message? Why me? 'Cause God was doing a new thing.

It didn't start in that church in Los Angeles. That was just the first time I said out loud what I had to do. Before then, I was wondering: What did that church have to do with the church in New York? And why was that white guy in the airport asking if I was a preacher? That young girl, Michelle, who said God told her to tell me to get out while I still can? This was all within the span of two days. That was no coincidence.

Everywhere I went people were walking up, saying, "Yo, I'm

praying for you." Tia and Tamara (the twins from the *Sister/Sister* TV show) were saying, "We're praying for you." Why are all these people praying for me? And then it became so clear.

When I left that church in Los Angeles, this guy ran up to me before I got out of the door. He said, "Yo, I hope what you said you're doing, you're serious about. A couple of days before Tupac got killed he was in this church talking about doing the same thing."

It was all too much for me. When I got back to New York I was still leery for a whole day. I didn't want to believe what was happening to me. But after a day, I picked up that Bible again and opened it up and it opened to the Book of Luke. Jesus was talking to the rich young ruler and he said, "You still lack one thing. Sell everything you have and give to the poor, and you will gain a treasure in heaven. Then come follow me."

Yeah, it was clear what I had to do. I was not going to run anymore.

"Get rid of everything and humble yourself so I can use you the way I need to," He said.

The first moment I started talking to God, it was clear what He was saying back to me.

Why wasn't I talking to Him all this time?

He knew I was seriously seeking Him.

And I said, "God, if you don't show me, I'm not going to make it. If you ain't serious, God, let me just stay over here. If you don't tell me exactly what I need to do, I can't do it. Just tell me what to do, God. And I promise you I'll do it."

I got on a plane and went to Atlanta. I don't even know why. When I got there, God told me to get rid of the Mercedes.

No, God, not the Mercedes!

God wouldn't be telling me to get rid of that. I just prayed about that one. And I kept getting the same answer—get rid of the car. I brought the title to the church that I started going to and just gave it to a person in the church. They couldn't believe it. They were so happy and it felt good to see that. There was a young lady in the church struggling in college. I gave her the diamonds out of my ears. I put them in her hands and said, "Be blessed."

But God was like, "You still didn't get rid of that chain, that ring, and that watch." I had given away one of my trucks and I held on to the other one. It ended up getting stolen and crashed. I lost the chain and the ring.

"Okay, God, I'm getting the message," I said.

I gave away the platinum bracelet and everything else. Everything I didn't give away, God somehow took from me. He sure knows how to get your attention.

When people saw me, I even looked different. They could see it.

"Ma$e, what's up?!" they would say. I couldn't answer them. I wasn't Ma$e anymore. They would see me without the jewelry and would say, "I think he's broke," or "Ma$e done sold out." But I wasn't broke. Shortly after I gave everything away God blessed me with everything. But what I thought was everything was nothing. And what I thought was nothing was everything. Everything to Ma$e was materialistic and that meant nothing to God. What I thought was nothing was peace. I thought happiness was nothing because you can't be happy without money. Nothing to Ma$e is freedom. And now I know that's everything.

Ma$e and Mason are two different people—two entirely different people. Mason is very intelligent. Mason can do anything he wants without the money. Ma$e needs the money, the jewelry, the clothes, the girls. Satan gave Ma$e all the things Mason would have gotten eventually anyway with God. Satan just gave it to Ma$e upfront.

Satan feared what Ma$e would change into if he learned the truth. Satan wanted to put up distractions and give a detour. And Ma$e took the road Satan offered. Ma$e didn't wait for God. So I had to get rid of everything Satan gave Ma$e. I had to cleanse myself of that. And God said, "Since you've done that for me, let me show you what I can do."

And what He's shown me is greater and bigger than anything Ma$e ever got.

Today I have my own ministry, my own church, S.A.N.E.—Saving A Nation Endangered Ministries. I want to reach people no one else can reach. I want to help people see God. Because God is definitely doing a new thing.

*If ye endure chastening, God dealeth with you as with sons;
for what son is he whom the father chasteneth not?*

*But if ye be without chastisement, where of all are
partakers, then are ye bastards, and not sons.*

—HEBREWS 12:7-8

Sermon

*T*oday what we're going to talk about is a message that God has placed in my heart for a very long time. The message is, "Hell is not full." I think a lot of people need to know that hell is never full in order for us to cross rivers and make transitions and take cities. Most of us who are living correctly need an incentive to keep doing so. The incentive is—Hell is not full. Just as God can do anything with a little bit, and God can do it with nothing. You need to know that hell is not full.

When I say hell is not full, it means there are some people who are empty spiritually. They are living a lifestyle that shows no spirituality. That's the time when you're most attacked—when you feel empty, when you feel like you have nothing. When you feel like a father's not there, so you have no emotion there, you have no financial stability there, no physical ability there. That's when Satan comes in and does his best work.

The Book of Proverbs was written by Solomon. Solomon was one of the wisest men of Israel. Solomon wasn't just a man who was a prophet, he also came from a prophet.

God wanted Solomon to teach the people the value of hard work. Through Solomon, he also wanted to teach people the value of obedience. He wanted to teach them the value of treating people right. He wanted to teach people to have compassion for the poor. He wanted to teach us the importance of family bonds. These are things today that we don't take too seriously.

(sermon continued on page 33)

In the Beginning

I was born early, almost two months early, on August 27, 1975. I guess from the very beginning I was coming onto the scene before people were ready for me.

I have a twin sister, Stason, and we are the youngest of six children—there's Sabrina, Michael, Anthony, Yolanda, Stason and me, Mason. My mother brought us up well. We always had. We knew it was a struggle for my mother, but she made sure we always had. We left Jacksonville, Florida, when Stason and I were three or four years old. We had to leave; my biological father wasn't right.

I would have to say I have the best mother in the world. My mother has a really big heart and she puts up with things she doesn't have to for a long time. You know how some people are so generous and so sweet, they just give you the benefit of the doubt hoping one day you'll do better. When I got older I would tell her, "People are trying to burn you out and use you up and when they don't have any more use for you they won't deal with you anymore." After seeing it for herself one too many times, she finally caught on.

And my biological father was one of those people who tried to burn her out and use her up.

We had to leave Jacksonville because my biological father was a little crazy. He was a wild dude. He would try to lock my moms in the house and tell her she couldn't talk to nobody. He would beat her for real, for real—with his fists. He was too crazy. My moms couldn't put him out—he was too much—so she had to leave. With certain people you just have to pack your stuff and go.

We took a train from Florida to New York. I don't remember much about what happened before we left, but I remember that train ride was real quiet and real long. Nobody was talking and we didn't know where we were going. My mother left with no money, just us kids and some clothes. We ended up staying with her brother, my uncle Leamon, who took care of us until my mother was able to get on her feet.

And she got on her feet quickly.

My mother taught me about perseverance and fighting through adversity. She says I get some of my expressions and my stubbornness from my father. When I decide to do something, that's it, there's no changing my mind. And she says my father was like that, too. But I never experienced that first-hand.

But I know I'm stubborn. No matter what anyone would tell me, if I was determined, they had to get out of the way. When I decided I wanted to be a rapper, I meant it. No matter how many people told me I was crazy, I kept trying. And I did make it. After that my mother said, "I see so much in you. I think you're going to be able to break the curse." There's a curse in being the way my father was. There's a curse in being so willful that you can't do right. My mother said that I would be able to use that strong personality for good things. "Instead of leaving your kids, you're going to be good," she said. "You're going to do good things."

I believe him not being in my life inspired me to do something great. I used his absence as energy to make something happen. It's almost like someone telling you you can't do something. Not growing up with your father around can be like a strike against you, but I used it as fuel. It made me push harder to be better—be better than he was.

The summer after my senior year in high school was one of the worst. It was supposed to be the summer I graduated from high school. But I found out during the last month that I would have to repeat the twelfth grade. I missed too many days of school. And, as if that wasn't enough, my moms was constantly on my back about school and getting a job.

That summer it also seemed like all of my friends were getting killed. Tyrone Lineburger was murdered. He was shot in the throat. Butch was killed right along with him. Tyrone was one of my best friends. He looked out for me. He was small, but people were scared of him. You know how the small dudes have to make an impression on the streets, and Tyrone who had a lot of heart, definitely had built a reputation. And Butch was a big guy—he was Tyrone's sidekick.

They both used to hustle drugs. I would want to tag along with them, but they wouldn't let me. With them, I was always looked at as "the one"—the one who was going to make it— and they didn't want me in trouble. "He's the one who will go somewhere," they used to say. "He's going to get some real money one day."

While doing a deal, they both got killed. In the drug game you need heart, muscle, and money to make it. You can have money, but no respect, and that isn't good. And if you only have heart and muscle, the people can have something done to you. Tyrone and Butch had heart and muscle but no money. And somebody got something done to them.

Michael Duncan, another close friend, died in a car accident. A few weeks later, Kenneth got shot going in a drive-through to get something to eat at a Wendy's. I grew up with Kenneth and Michael. We started playing basketball together at P.S. 175 and continued in the neighborhood. Kenneth and Michael were hustle players—you could count on them for tight defense, steals, and just wreaking havoc on the courts.

With so many of my friends dying, I became closer to new people like Cameron Giles, Richie Parker, and Andre Thompson. We played together on the basketball team during my first senior year at Manhattan Center High School and made it all the way to the PSAL Finals. We lost, but we were the baddest team in the city.

But none of it was the same without Kenneth and Michael. Their only crime was being at the wrong place at the wrong time.

And while everybody seemed to be dying around me, I was getting calls from girls talking about, "I'm pregnant."

I was a young, wild dude—an average young, wild guy from Harlem, New York. All of us played ball, liked to party, and liked women. I just kept getting caught out there.

I got caught out there for the first time when I was sixteen. I was with this girl who lived in the apartment next door. I would slip in there on the regular when her moms went to work and would take care of my business. It was real convenient going over there just about every day, until she came to me with "I'm pregnant!"

"Oh, no!" I said. I was real scared, and so was she. She was only fifteen and neither one of us were ready for a baby. My first senior year in high school? That was *not* the life! She got rid of it and I paid for it.

"The next time," I thought. "I'm gonna be real careful." From that day on, I started using rubbers. But sometimes rubbers don't always do the job—especially when they break. I got snagged again trying to protect my reputation—maybe a little too much—and I ripped right through a Trojan, extra large. Pregnancy number two.

This one was different, though. I really liked this young lady who lived in the Bronx. She was special, real smart. Maybe I really liked her because she was the first girl I took time to know. She was a virgin and we hung out for a year before we slept together. We were both seventeen and I was with her all the way through my first senior year and into my second. But Ma$e being Ma$e, I eventually cracked the code, got in, and downloaded. But she was the most innocent girl I had ever been with, and I liked that.

And her family was real cool. Her mother loved me and her aunt made the best pound cake in the world.

She had a bright future. She wanted to be a doctor, and I knew a baby would ruin it. She had an abortion. After her, there were a few more girls who said they were pregnant. But everybody seemed to be playing pregnant to get abortion money. I was just happy to know it worked out for all of us.

Then there was my mother. She was really getting on me

to get a job. I finally got a job at Bay Plaza in the Bronx, at a movie theatre. But I got fired the first day. They had me in this uniform; they had me wearing their colors—some black jeans and a royal blue polo shirt that said BAY PLAZA CINEMAS. And that wasn't my style at all. I was an usher and that meant that any customer who wanted could come up and ask me a bunch of questions.

My girlfriend—my main girl—stopped by to chill with me, and while we were talking, this dude kept coming up to me telling me he needed this or he needed that. He was bothering me all day and threatening to get the manager because I wasn't moving fast enough for him. And he's doing this in front of my girl.

He can't be serious!

Since I had never worked before, I didn't understand all of that about the customer always being right. I didn't understand that people could just be rude and you had to take it. That they could talk to you any old kind of way and you shouldn't answer back. I wasn't having it.

When this dude came back acting real stupid, getting loud and rude, I just looked at him.

You don't know how bad I don't want to work here anyway; please say the wrong thing.

And he did.

I was like, "For real?" I was calm. That's the way I always was, even in school. Kids used to try to pick fights with me because they thought it was hilarious when I got mad. They really wanted to see if I would talk faster. My expression never changed and I never raised my voice or got excited, even while I was fighting.

I said to this dude, "Yo, let me change my clothes. You're gonna be right here when I get back, right?" I went to change my uniform because I was going to hurt this guy. When I got outside to meet him, the manager told me not to come back. That was crazy. In a way I was happy. I only got the job to get my mother off my back.

I was just going through it. And with all that I was going through—my friends dying, my mother getting on me about getting a job, the abortions—it was like nothing really mattered anymore. I lost my emotions—my ability to feel.

My mother was real disappointed in how I was acting. She'd say, "I hope you plan on getting out of high school." But I didn't really care about nothing. I was trying, for her. But it wasn't working out. I even tried to hustle once. I was supposed to be working out of this abandoned building with this kid. When I got there, the kid told me all the money got burned up 'cause the whole building caught on fire. Like I'm stupid. But I took it as a sign. Things I would try that weren't right? As soon as I tried them, something would go wrong. Just to let me know, it wasn't for me.

I also had gotten involved with holding somebody's money once while they hustled. And I got robbed. The only thing that saved me from getting hurt was my reputation. Actually it was the reputation of my brothers—Ant (short for Anthony) and Mike. Both of them were known on the streets for being crazy. They would go haywire. They were time bombs just waiting to explode—the type of dudes who would get mad, break people's windows and throw garbage cans. They would even take drugs from drug dealers and never returned with their money. And nothing would happen to them.

So nobody messed with me.

When I told those drug dealers that I was robbed all they said to me was, "Yo, Shorty, you have to be more careful because people can get hurt." Another one said, "That guy, Ma$e, he's cool. He doesn't need to be out there anyway." They never asked me to get involved in their business again.

I made it through my first senior year—still getting into trouble. I was doing petty things.

We were only passing in school to play ball. And there were some cool teachers who would give me a 65 just because I was on the basketball team and we were winning a lot of games. A *lot* of games. We made it all the way to the PSAL championship where we lost to Brandeis.

After basketball season was over, my grades dropped and I cut class a lot and that's why I got left back.

My second senior year there was no more basketball for me. They didn't let second-year seniors play so I had to find another form of entertainment. That year we would be gambling in the hallways—C-Lo and craps. It was like another curriculum for us.

And I had to make sure I passed enough to graduate this time. And I did—thanks to my boys and Pei Ming. She was the only Chinese student in the school and she had a 95 average. She couldn't go home with less than a 95. So on tests I made sure I sat next to Pei Ming, Kareem, or Andre, who we called "Dre."

By the end of the school year a few of the teachers got wise and started splitting us up. One teacher who caught me said, "Mason, I know someone who went cross-eyed doing that." But it didn't stop me. I needed to finish my second senior year.

That ended up being one of my best years in school as far as fun, especially hanging with Cam, Richie, and Dre, who were my best friends.

Dre was hilarious. He was the only one in our crew with a job. He worked in a bodega—the only black dude in a store full of Arabs. And we called him "Dre-dega" for the longest time. But during our second senior year, he got a new nickname.

He had saved up two thousand dollars over the summer and kept that money in cash in his pocket. When teachers would get on him to pay attention in class, Dre would whip out his two-thousand-dollar wad and say, "I don't need school, I got two thousand dollars!"

And it was a big thing for a high school student to have that kind of money. Our senior trip was two hundred dollars and most of the kids were struggling to scrape that together. But Dre had two thousand dollars.

If he got into an argument with another student, he would pull out his money and say, "I got two thousand dollars. Discussion over!" It was hilarious, and got to the point when people who got into an argument knew how it would end and would beat him to the punch, "Yeah, yeah, Dre, we know, we know, you got two thousand dollars."

We started calling him "Dre 2000." And it stuck. That was my boy. He would take care of me. When he had loot, he would take me out to eat, buy me gear, or we would go to clubs. And he never left his stash drop below that two thousand dollars. If he had to work for a month to save an extra eight hundred dollars to play with, he would. One week he would have new Jordans and that same two thousand dollars.

He would buy a new leather jacket the next week and never put a dent in that two thousand dollars. Today he probably has an apartment and a car—and that same two thousand dollars.

He was a character.

So was Cam. He was different from Dre, more reserved and a little smoother. We had played ball together for like forever. But during my second senior year we just took our friendship to a new level. Me and Cam always talked about making it big. We would be NBA superstars.

We even started rapping together as a hobby and started a little rap group called Children of the Corn. The "corn" stood for "the corner." Damon Dash, who was just a student at Manhattan Center, was our manager. He even got us a gig in Long Island once but left us to chase after this other dude named Big L, who he felt was really going to make it.

Me and Cam were inseparable. We would always talk about what we were going to do when we got rich. We said that no matter what, nothing would separate our friendship. Ironically, we did finally make it. We got into music and went in totally opposite directions. Isn't that funny . . .

Me, Dre, Cam, and Richie were always into something. Our school was right in the community, off the FDR, right near the projects. So whatever happened in school usually spilled out into the neighborhood. That was cool, because our boys who didn't go to Manhattan Center but lived in the neighborhood would be right there after school for any festivities we had planned.

We would have water fights after school, trying to get the girls' tops wet for our own private wet T-shirt contest. We even devised this money-making scheme. Our school was selling raffle tickets, so we printed up our own and were selling them for a dollar. The school was selling theirs for three. So everybody was buying ours. Of course, we got caught because we were greedy. We always got caught, especially Cam and me.

Everyone got caught, except for Richie—he was the star of our basketball team. While me and Cam were getting suspended, Richie would be laughing. He'd be dropping 35 in the next game. So the one time he *did* get caught kind of made up for all of the times me and Cam got in trouble combined.

Richie was caught up in a rape scandal in our school. This girl accused him and a couple of other dudes of forcing her to perform oral sex in a stairwell. She was a freshman or a sophomore—and bilingual. I never knew that cutting school would pay off. Me and Cam didn't go that day, which was a blessing because it is very likely that we would have been in that hallway with Richie.

It was real bad for Rich. That ruined any chances he had of going pro. He never got into a major college to play ball and that was kind of it for him.

The only rough part of my second senior year was that I couldn't play ball. And I hated going to class. I thought about dropping out. But Mrs. Shineback saved me. She was the guidance counselor who took an interest in me. She was so sweet. She said, "Mason, we're going to get you into college." She signed me up for the special-funding program, which was for students who couldn't afford college tuition. So I got to go to college for free. I got into SUNY Purchase in Westchester, New York. Perfect. That's where the Knicks practiced, and I already told you I thought I was going to the NBA one day.

I went through the summer program on the campus of

SUNY Purchase and ended up the valedictorian. Now *that* was crazy—from being left back to being head of the class. Mrs. Shineback was moved. "Nobody ever said you were stupid. I knew what you could do if you only applied yourself." All I had to do up there was study and play basketball. All my boys had basically gone their own way. Cam was at a junior college in Fort Worth, Texas. Dre was going to school and working all the time—increasing that two thousand dollars in his pocket.

I was looking forward to playing ball on the college level and I knew my game was ready. But after my first couple of games at SUNY I knew there would be trouble. The coach took me out and I sat on the bench a lot. The coach said I was too flashy. He said I was playing to the crowd. I tried to play the way he wanted me to play but we only ended up winning five games.

I said to him, "If you let me be me, we'll win. Either let me play the way I want to play or I'm not playing at all." He kicked me off the team.

That summer I came home and I saw everybody outside and it was like nobody was doing anything different from the previous summer. Everyone was still doing the same thing on the same corner with the same girls, talking about the same stuff. That was boring to me.

I went back up to SUNY and just spent my days in the gym playing pick-up games and shooting around. I met this guy, Derek Harper, who played point guard for the Knicks. I was shooting three-pointers in the gym and I said to him, "I'm the best. Nobody want no parts of me out here."

He said, "Yeah, yeah, wait till my boy comes." He was talking about Charlie Ward. Derek swore up and down that Charlie Ward could check me.

"Tell your boy to come," I said. "Tell him to hurry up before the ambulance comes because I'm killing them out here." I pulled up for a three and said to Derek, "Watch, this could be you." Swish! Growing up in New York, I didn't respect Knicks players.

"I bet you two hundred dollars you can't make fifteen baskets in a row from each side of the elbow," he said. A piece of cake. I said, "You better have that money ready."

Clang! Clang!

I kept missing and didn't get that two hundred dollars. But I kept coming back. I was practicing all week. When I saw Derek I would say, "I'm going to get that money." And I did. I finally made those fifteen shots in a row.

Soon we became real cool. He used to let me drive his Benz—a white SL.

This joint is fast.

We went to get something to eat, which was a nice break from the Oodles of Noodles diet I was on. He took me under his wing. He would even give me money from time to time.

What have I got to do for this money?

I was always taught that if you got money from somebody, they were going to want something in return.

He told me that God wanted him to look out for me, be a big brother to me while I was in college because, "One day you will do it for someone else."

He got me into working out—not just on my game but in the weight room. When I first got to SUNY, I was really, really, skinny. I was a toothpick, but I was very quick. Nobody could stop me I was so fast.

By the end of the summer Derek said, "Looks like you put on a few pounds." I said, "Yeah, I'm getting into pro shape."

I was really going to tear up that rinky-dink conference we were in. But that coach was being strict. He wouldn't let me play my game.

I said, "This ain't the life." So I didn't get to play again. He wanted me to play his system. But that system didn't work.

Derek said he was going to try to get me into Illinois University. But I was through with my hoop dreams. Through with basketball and college. I was only in school really for basketball and if I couldn't play, I wasn't interested.

Go to school to work for somebody? That ain't the life.

So I was spending most of my days when I wasn't in the gym back in my room getting high. I was living in a three-bedroom suite on campus with this Spanish dude named Lou, a Chinese kid named Henry, an African guy named Topsy, and this six-foot-seven dude from Brooklyn named Curtis. It was crazy—like the United Nations up in there.

I shared a room with Curtis. He was so tall that I would constantly bump into his legs in the morning on my way to the bathroom. So we set up our bunk beds the way Arnold and Willis had theirs on *Diff'rent Strokes*. Topsy was so tall we had to put the two tall dressers at the end of his bed so he could fit.

After classes—if we went at all—we would all be sitting in the living room, blasting Raekwon's *Only Built 4 Cuban Link* real loud, smoking weed. One day, right in the middle of the school year, we were in the living room smoking and I said, "I need to get up out of here. This ain't the life for me." I still felt that when I came off my high. I went back to Harlem. I decided I was going to become a rapper.

When I got home, I told my mother my plans. She said, "You dropping out to rap? If you ain't gonna go to school you can't stay here."

So I was on the streets.

I moved in with my twin sister, Stason, on 133rd Street between Lenox and Seventh Avenues. She got pregnant when she was sixteen and had a baby. She finished school and got her own apartment. She had a job and was doing really well for herself. She let me stay with her but told me, "Don't be bringing all them girls into my house." I didn't listen. Eventually I had to move from there too. Actually, she never told me to leave. My sister had a way of making herself clear without saying a word—through her facial expressions. I just knew it was time to leave.

I really didn't have anyplace to go. And I didn't have any money. But inside, I felt like the richest man in the world without a dime to my name. I was waiting on a miracle to happen. At least what I thought would be a miracle. I already knew I was going to be something. There wasn't no way that I was *not* going to be something.

Around that time I met Cooda. And everything began to change.

The father of the righteous shall greatly rejoice: and he that begetteth a wise child *shall have joy of him.*

—PROVERBS 23:24

Sermon

*G*od also used Solomon to show how he could take the foolish things of the world and teach people to be wise. The thing that made Solomon great was that he was more concerned with divine things—concerned with studying the divine things. He wanted to talk about the divine things; he wanted to be about the divine thing. When he wrote The Scripture he specifically said hell and destruction are never full. Solomon knew it was important to do the things that God wanted him to do, even though he could have used his wisdom for many other things.

When I first started attending church regularly, my pastor allowed me to come in shorts and jeans and boots. He also allowed me to sit in the pulpit, because Moses' era is over and it was about a new thing. But God used his wisdom to be able to teach me and because he chose to use his wisdom, I want my pastor to know that God is going to honor that. Out of all the ways he could have taken me, he used his wisdom for the right things. Out of all the things he could have gotten out of me, knowing I was vulnerable and wanting to know God, he could have done so many things, but he did the right things and God is going to honor wisdom in these last days.

So with Solomon—he could have used his wisdom for his kingdom, for his purpose, whatever he wanted to do, but he chose to use it to transmit posterity for the people. Now posterity is different than prosperity.

Posterity means I am going to grow successfully. Everything I grow into will be successful. What I want young people to have is posterity—not prosperity. Most people want to be prosperous instead of having posterity—everything you do when you're growing in God is going to be successful. So I rather have posterity. Prosperity will come and go.

(sermon continued on page 59)

THREE

The Magic Dragon

One Hundred and Thirty-ninth Street. That was the spot. That was where I first caught the rapping bug. Me and Cam and Dre would be out there rapping after school and all summer long. I would make up raps on the spot and folks would be *oohing* and *ahhing*, saying, "That boy's going to be nasty."

This was 1994, and I think Wu Tang had just come out. We were into them, but we would say if we ever got a record deal, we were going to be better. We thought we looked better and we thought our rhymes were tighter.

Back then, nobody was really serious about breaking into the rap game. Me and my boys thought we were going to the NBA. Rap was just a hobby for all of us, except Big L. He would be on that corner every day, too. And he actually ended up with a record deal with Columbia. He was going to be huge. That was a bad boy.

Big L, whose name was Lamont, was circulating his first single on tape and it was hot. He used the sample from an old DeBarge song. Somebody must have heard "It" because Bad

Boy ended up with the rights to the sample and that was all she wrote. Biggie released "One More Chance" with the exact same sample. That joint went platinum. Biggie became a huge star. And Big L's career was over before it even started.

But Big L was still out there on 139th Street and Lenox Avenue, rapping. We all were. That was the rapping corner, the same corner as the twenty-four-hour chicken joint. There was a park where we would ball every day until three in morning. And there was a bunch of money being made over there—hustling and gambling. There was some of everything going on on 139th and Lenox.

In addition to rapping and balling, I also did some gambling in an abandoned building on the corner. One day while doing my thing, this lady came up to us. She seemed like she was drunk.

She said to us, "If you could just live until Saturday, you're gonna be blessed." It was Monday and Saturday seemed like a long time away. She also said, "Basically these are the instructions: Don't cross no bridges. And don't get in nobody's car."

Man, I can't do this!

My moms had just moved to Mount Vernon. And I had to be in Harlem. I didn't know anybody in Mount Vernon and wasn't nothing happening up there. It was so far; I couldn't even get a chick to come up there. They weren't getting on a train at 145th to go all the way up to 241st and then walk ten blocks or catch a dollar cab to Moms' place.

But I couldn't forget what that lady had told me. "Don't cross no bridges. Don't get in nobody's car."

It was impossible for me to get back and forth without getting in a car or crossing a bridge. So I had to stay in Harlem at my sister's place until Saturday. And if I had any ideas about leaving, I was convinced not to when one of my boys died across a bridge. I kid you not, within a week, my boy Derrick, who we called Blood, got killed in a car crash going under the bridge under 155th Street, near the Rucker.

That week Blood came to my sister's house and said, "My pops bought me a brand new BMW." Cameron was there begging me to come downstairs and go for a ride, but I wouldn't. And they laughed at me.

"You always so scared on that spirit tip," Cameron said.

Blood ended up dying in that car his father bought when he crashed it on the bridge over 155th Street, near the Rucker.

The lady also told my boy Chili that day, "You always worried about how you gonna have money. You stay with him and you gonna be blessed."

She was telling Chili to stick close to me and she told him not to go to the East Side. She told him, "You got this dark-skinned friend and y'all will both get killed if you go to the East Side. I want you to go home and apologize to your mother because she's about to put you out."

Chili was really freaked out. Chili's friend did get killed during that same month. And he didn't stick by me. He ended up in jail. The Saturday after the lady told me I would be blessed, I was in Atlanta getting ready to be signed.

I met Puffy in Atlanta at the Hard Rock Cafe on Peachtree Street downtown. They were holding an after-party there for a rap convention where everybody who ever thought about being in the rap business—and every big shot who could put them down—was there.

I had to be there, too.

Cooda is a guy I would say is a survivor. He's one of those dudes who good things always happened to. In a way he's like me. He is a real good-hearted dude and whatever he was into, he made something happen. He always ended up where he had to be. He was Biggie's road manager. I don't even know how he got to be Biggie's road manager or even where he came from. He went to one of those Virginia state colleges, but nobody knew where he was from. They just knew him. Nobody knew his real name. Everybody knew Cooda from somewhere different—but no one knew where he was from.

I met Cooda through my twin sister, Stason. He was dating a girl named Jeanine who was a really good friend of my sister. He was all in love with her and wherever you saw Jeanine, you saw Cooda's concern. My only assumption is that maybe he was afraid that somebody was going to take her. Stason told Cooda about me. "Yo, you've got to meet my brother!" she told him, and gave him this tape I made. Stason was always my biggest fan.

After hearing the tape, he came up to SUNY Purchase where I was going to school. He was with his boys Black Fred and Meat, who weighed a little more than three hundred pounds and traveled everywhere with Cooda.

"I already know you're nice," Cooda said. "I just need to know if you want to make money?"

"What?!" I said. "I'm down!"

"I'm gonna get you a deal," he said.

"Yeah, right!" I said. "That's what everybody says." But Cooda meant it.

He took me to Ron G's house in Manhattan. Ron G was a

popular club deejay. I rapped for Ron G and he was loving it. I didn't know where it was going, but I figured if Cooda was affiliated with Biggie and all these people, he must know something. That's all I was looking for—a chance. I knew one day the talent would show for itself. I just needed a place to showcase it.

The next week, Cooda had me rapping in front of Biggie. He was parked in a dark-green LandCruiser on 125th Street in Harlem, in front of the Apollo Theater. Biggie was sitting in the passenger side with a tape blasting from his system. I was on the sidewalk, wearing a Tommy Hilfiger raincoat, a Nautica snow hat, and a hoodie to try and keep warm. It was like 30 degrees. I was freezing and freestyling for him, right there on the street.

When I was done, Biggie said, "I like Shorty." He wanted to put me down with this group he had started called Junior M.A.F.I.A. But I told him that I didn't really want to be a part of a group. He wanted to keep me around anyway. He would give me backstage passes to his shows in New York City and Long Island. I loved it—all the excitement, all the chicks.

I would meet chicks back then and when they weren't feeling me, I would say, "Keep acting funny, you're gonna know who I am in a minute."

And they would say, "What's up with that little boy?"

I was nineteen, but I knew where I was going to be. I was going to be rich. I was going to be a star. I was going to live that life.

I would say to those chicks, "I'm Ma$e. Remember my name."

Six months later, everybody knew my name.

Cooda made that happen. He looked after me. He even took me in after I left my sister's house. That's the kind of dude he was. Cooda lived on 123rd and 7th Avenue in a one-bedroom apartment with a mattress and a sleeping bag in the living room. At any given time there would be four or five dudes sleeping in that tiny apartment.

We didn't care. We would be up all hours planning and plotting, eating White Castle every night—usually the cheeseburgers. And when I thought I was feeling bourgie, I would order the chicken sandwich. I didn't have any money, but somehow every night I was eating.

Cooda sold his Acura Legend and we put aside money for the plane tickets, and with the rest he took me shopping. You can't go anywhere trying to impress people looking any old kind of way. I had to stand out. All those big-shot dudes were concerned with how you look, what you're wearing.

I don't know how we got to Atlanta; nobody had any money for traveling. But Cooda knew and I knew I had to be there. Coming out of that convention with people talking about me was all the buzz I needed. Most people put their stuff on a tape and went around shopping it to whoever they could get to listen. I never wanted to do that. I had to do my thing in person, live. They either got to hear me in person or not at all. I always believed if I could do it in person, they would have no choice but to sign me. And in Atlanta, I would have that chance.

So I made sure I looked the part. Cooda lent me his Versace shirt. It was silk and rayon with these crazy colors. I bought some Versace shoes and pants. I stood in front of the Hard Rock Cafe in Atlanta in this outfit—frontin' in another man's shirt—thinking you can't tell me nothing. Somebody's going to notice me. We're getting in.

I had shown out the whole day at the convention, rapping for anybody who would hear me and folks were already starting to talk. "Yo, that kid's nice!" they were saying.

But we were still outside this joint while everyone else— the ones who can make a deal happen for me—were inside.

Jermaine Dupree pulled up in some expensive car and they had his name in the sky in Batman lights. Cooda tried to talk to him as he was going in but his bodyguards stopped him.

Then we saw Mark Pitts, who was Biggie's manager. He had just gotten his own label and was cool with Cooda. He knew about me and liked me but he had just signed Tracy Lee and wasn't looking for another rapper for a while. But he got us in the party.

When we got in, me and Cooda headed for the VIP section. We tried to grab Kris Kross who were right by Jermaine Dupree. But they were looking at us funny in the face, like they didn't want to hear us.

"All right! Y'all will know who I am!" I said. And the guards came over and said, "Chill, chill, Shorty. Back up from the barricade."

Cooda was able to get Puff's attention. He got behind the barricade, was talking in his ear, and pointed over to me.

Puffy came up to me and said, "Shorty, I'm gonna give you one chance. If you're good I'm a sign you. If you're not, I'm going to play you for wasting my time. So don't play yourself. Whatever you got, give it."

He ain't say nothing but a word. I gave him all I had right there in the club. I did a verse similar to the one heard on

112's "Only You." And Puff started doing his dance and everything right in the middle of the dance floor. And when I was done, it was over. I knew it. He knew it. And the whole club knew it. I could see it in his face that he was impressed.

He said, "You rap like that all the time? That slow?" I told him that was my style. He told me I reminded him of this kid he signed name Jadakiss.

He told Cooda, "When you get back to New York, don't talk to anyone. Come straight to my office and I will sign Shorty."

We get back to New York and Cooda's phone was ringing off the hook. Heavy D and everybody at Uptown wanted to talk to me now. Damon Dash, my fake high school manager, now had his own label, Rockafella. He wanted to holler at me. And so did the folks at Tommy Boy. They figured if Puff wanted to sign me, then I must be nice.

We listened to everybody. We went to meet with Heavy D, who was the head of Uptown Records. Heavy had just signed this group, So For Real, that was blowing up. And he was interested in signing me, too.

So we sat down and one of the first things he said was, "We have got to do something about your look." He said I was an average brown-skinned dude and I had to stand out. But I was trying to get him to see that I had the frenzy already. I had a look.

He was talking about wanting me to grow an Afro or something.

An Afro?! You just done bumped your head.

Strike one. But I kept listening. He also said that I could

be in a group with CL Smooth. Nah, man, that ain't me. I can't do a group. Strike two.

Then he started talking money. That's what I wanted to hear. He was throwing around numbers like $100,000 and $125,000 and I didn't like what I was hearing. I'm already thinking "millions." Strike three. We were out.

We finally went to see Puffy at Bad Boy. Before we even went there I had already felt in my heart that the best thing to do was go with Bad Boy. I was something they didn't have, and at the time Bad Boy was the hottest label. For me, it was like being drafted by Chicago during the Michael Jordan era or the Yankees in the 1990s or the Lakers today. They already had Shaq and Phil and I would be Kobe. Biggie was Shaq, just dominating the game. Puff was Phil Jackson, orchestrating all the success. And I was Kobe—versatile and marketable. How could I lose?

We met with Puffy at his office downtown. I had on my good outfit—a Tommy raincoat, a Nautica hat, a blue, maroon and white Tommy shirt, somebody else's boots. They were Timberlands that I borrowed from Cam. I always used to rock Cam's gear. He was the flyest dude in school and we wore the same size. We used to always switch clothes and boots. If he got something new he would let me rock it the next week. If I got something new, he could borrow it. But I ended up borrowing from him more because it seemed like he was always getting new stuff.

I was sitting there with Cooda, a little nervous because I didn't know exactly what to expect. Puffy was talking about me being the next thing.

He said, "Whatever you want to be, you can be at Bad Boy." He told me to listen to him and don't ask any questions. "I'm going to make you rich." I liked that system. There was nothing to talk about; just get paid.

All I remember is that at some point, Puffy slid this check over the table. It was for $50,000. The deal was for $250,000 with $50,000 up front.

Me and Cooda left that office and went straight to the bank—Chase Manhattan on 125th Street and 8th Avenue—to cash that joint. We were able to get half of the money right then. I told them, "It's Friday and I need my money. And if I can't have half, I going to take my account elsewhere." And I didn't even have an account with them.

And you know how people get, how they start acting funny when they get a little money. Well, I was no different. I was nineteen with $25,000 in my pocket and you know I lost my mind shopping. I gave Cooda $5,000 and I kept $20,000 for myself. We were running around buying everything. I bought a chain with the Virgin Mary on it for $3,000. I bought three Avirex jackets, a bunch of Tims, a Northface. I was getting my wardrobe together first. Then I went to my neighborhood and picked all my boys up. They were like, "Yo, son, what happened!" I said, "I signed! I'm a star!!"

"Say word!" Dre said. "That's it, I'm rolling with you!"

Dre 2000 said he was dropping out of South Carolina State. "I don't need to go to school no more, right? Remember me, Dre 2000?"

I brought my boys to Jimmy Jazz on 125th and me and Dre were laughing, talking about "Lock the door! We're going to buy the store!"

I said, "Everybody, get what you want!" It was one of the best feelings in the world to be able to do that for your boys and be able to buy stuff for your sister and say, "Here, give this to my niece and toss her some dough." To be able to say, "Mom, take this," and give her a ring and make sure she had money. That was nice.

But she was a little skeptical when I first came home with a handful of jewelry. She said, "Boy, don't come in here with that hot stuff!"

"Mom, please!" I said. "It ain't hot. I just signed a record deal."

I tried to spend every dollar I had over that weekend. If I left the bank with the whole $50,000, I might have spent that too. "Why are we saving?" I thought. "There's plenty more where that came from."

And more checks were coming. And more money was being spent. I bought a brand new BMW, a silver 318. At first I would go down to Tito's in the diamond district. But when the money really started flowing, I went down to Jacob's and bought everybody in my crew a Rolex or a chain. If you were with me, you got something. If I shopped and you were with me, you got something. We were rolling now. At that point I could buy ten Rolex watches—the $15,000 Presidential—and tell them to send an invoice to my accountant.

I started writing music for other people. I wrote "Crush on You" for Biggie. That's where I got the money for the BMW. It was just on from there; it took off. There was no waiting process. After I signed, I was put to work and making money.

When "Only You" did well, Puff said, "Yo, we've got to do an album together!"

The first single, "Can't Nobody Hold Me Down" was #1 for twenty-five weeks on *Billboard*. Everybody was like, "Yo, this kid must be Midas." Brian McKnight called and said he wanted to do a song with me.

Brian McKnight? Yo, I'm about to turn this joint out! It's me, I'm the one! Ya'll are just role players. But I'm the one!

That was my mind set. Everybody was just playing. But I'm the one! I got a little trainer and started working out. I threw on a white tank top and it was about to get ugly. Everybody was calling for me and I was getting a minimum of a hundred thousand per song. No more talking, and I needed my money before we even talked about going into the studio. Many of the people calling me now were the same ones who weren't interested in signing me. These were the same dudes who were signing artists who didn't even make it and putting me on the back burner. Now they had to pay.

It was nothing personal, it was just business. So just send me my money.

And Cooda was right there helping me collect and making things happen. He was there spending money with me and helping me make more money. We used to buy cars together, buy jewelry together, and pick up girls together.

And every other weekend he would have us in some small town doing a show. Just for the money. Cooda would go into a small town and get them all excited about me coming. It was wild because at the time, I only had half a song, the rap part of 112's "Only You." But Cooda was milking that for all it was worth.

He got me my first gig in this tiny club in North Carolina. This joint was so small that I was rapping with a mic from the turntables with the cord coming from the mixer. There was a little roped off area in front of the deejay's table that was supposed to separate me from the crowd. But the crowd was so close I could smell their breath.

It was crazy. I did my rap from "Only You" and the rest of the night I freestyled over beats and we turned that club out. We made twelve hundred dollars, which we split fifty-fifty and I think we spent it all before we even got back to New York. We didn't care. We were having fun and we were on the road.

I was riding high—until one day I got a call from Cooda who told me we were broke.

"What?!" I said. "I ain't buying that." He told me he went to the bank and was told that everything was gone. I had hired a lawyer to watch over all the money that was coming in. Cooda picked me up and we went to this lawyer's office on 28th Street on the East Side of Manhattan and he was gone. His name on the door was gone and his office was cleaned out. We found out he ran away to Brazil with everything.

That hurt a lot. There was nothing we could do. We had to start over from scratch. This just made me more hungry. I called my boy, Tone, who had recently gotten a label called Wanna Blow, and I borrowed ten thousand until I got back on my feet. He gave me some money so I could live. I didn't want to ask Puffy for any money. I just felt that would be bad business. I'm not a leech. I needed my own money. And he had done enough.

Puffy moved me from Harlem to his apartment. At the time we were recording *No Way Out* and I was already rolling like a star. He didn't want me to get in any trouble staying in

Harlem. He knew people were hating on me and he didn't see it as a good situation. Neither did I.

You know how it goes down in the hood. When you have money, you either have to kill or be killed. Or you just have to leave. It is not about being scared; it's about making a wise decision. As much as you try to keep it real, a broke dude ain't got nothing to lose by trying to take what you got. And if you think for any reason a person won't point you out in a crowd, you couldn't be more wrong. People feel why you, out of everybody, was the one to make it. The guys see you as this young dude whose girl is comparing him to you. Or whose kids are looking up to you.

I would buy little kids ice cream in the park and their father would come up to me and say, "Yo, don't be giving my daughter money!" It was so crazy.

I had a kid's day in 145th Park with balloons and face painting, clowns, free food, and the whole yard. I didn't do it for the adults or for them to thank me but I was a little surprised when someone asked, "Who painted my son's face?" and was angry. It was like, "This guy, Mase. He doesn't stop. He doesn't quit." They felt like I was showing them up or showing off.

But it was only envy and jealousy. And those emotions make you do some crazy things.

The summer after I signed, I was still hanging out in my usual places. I was still going to the Rucker to watch the ball players. I was still hanging in the parks with my boys, smoking and snapping. One of my dogs was Shamgod Wells. He had just signed to play with the Washington Wizards.

The summer before we had gotten into a fight at 139th Park while we were hooping. We would be there from nine in the morning until nine at night just balling. He was good, but I would always handle my business against him. There would be battles out there.

So we got into it one night. "You ain't gonna be no rapper!" he said.

And I came back with, "You ain't gonna be in the NBA, you fake Isiah Thomas!"

He said, "You ain't no Biggie!" And it went back and forth like that for a while.

"Well, don't say nothing to me when I make it first," I said.

"And you don't say nothing to me when I make it!" he said. "You gonna be the first one riding me when I do."

And by the next summer we were both wrong. We both made it and we were friends, laughing about the summer before.

Me and Sham were standing on the corner of 142nd Street and Seventh Avenue just chilling when this Spanish dude comes up and asks us for change for a dollar. Before we could respond he took two steps, spun, and pulled out a gun. He put it right at Sham's head.

"Take off everything!" he said to me and Sham. "I'm gonna kill y'all anyway, but give me your stuff first."

In my head I was like, "I'm already around the corner!" I could run. And the guy must have seen me two-stepping because he said to Sham, "If he runs, I'm a pop you right now."

"Take off that watch!" he said to me. I had just bought a new Rolex the day before. So I said, "Man, I'll give you this chain, but I just got this watch."

I'm saying to myself, He might to just pop me once to show me he's serious.

He said, "I'm gonna murder you anyway." So I threw the watch on the ground because I knew he was serious and kicked it toward him. And when he bent over to get it, I yelled, "Sham, run!" And we were out. As we rounded the corner, there was a cop car there and they caught that dude. I wasn't worried about getting my stuff back. I had enough money to buy new stuff. But I could have died that day—being in the wrong place at the wrong time.

It was just another indication that I couldn't be at the places I used to go and do the things I used to do.

Every time I would show up at the basketball games at 155th at the Rucker, I could feel people watching me. I could see the hatred in the eyes of the people who were smiling.

They used to think, "What did I do?" or "He ain't so special."

It's like money creates space. People say you act funny when you get money—but it's really them who are acting funny. You're not acting funny because you don't eat Popeye's, White Castle, or McDonalds anymore. You just have better choices. But people feel like you're acting funny. They say, "Oh, he acts like he doesn't want to drink with us anymore."

I'm not acting funny. I just don't drink St. Ides because I don't have to. It's like everything upgrades and the people who can't upgrade hate you.

That's across the board. It ain't just black people. It ain't just in the hood. Sometimes I would go to a fancy restaurant and jump out and have the car valet parked and some people who weren't black would look at me and I could see what they were thinking, "How is this person so young able to afford that Mercedes?"

I was glad when Puff offered to let me stay at his apartment. The day I left the area of Harlem I was living in was a great feeling. It was like Israel leaving Egypt for me. I never felt like that life was for me. Whether I made it in music or basketball or business, I always knew I would be leaving Harlem. Wherever I was going to be, it wouldn't be in Harlem.

I was like the Jeffersons—moving on up to the East Side. Except it was downtown in the 30s. I threw what little bit of stuff I had into two duffel bags. I put them in a Touch of Class gypsy cab and I just rolled out.

I pulled up to Puffy's townhouse and it felt like that scene when Will Smith showed up in Beverly Hills for the first time in the *Fresh Prince of Bel Air.* The air even smelled different here. The streets were clean and there was order.

Puffy lived in a townhouse with a spiral staircase. His place was much different from Cooda's one bedroom with the dirty sleeping bags in the living room. Every room was huge. He had one room just for his clothes and he had a *lot* of clothes. He could wear an outfit only once and not run out of clothes in a year. And most of the time he did only wear stuff once. Lucky for me, we wore the same size—so every time he was finished with something, I got a whole new wardrobe.

Puffy would sometimes ask me, "How're you feeling?" He knew it had to be a big adjustment going from borrowing five dollars one day to having a hundred thousand the next. "I know it's probably going too fast but listen to me."

I was cool just rolling with him not realizing that he was trying to tell me that this was just the beginning. And I never questioned him—except when he wanted me to wear those shiny suits.

"I don't know about that," I said. "We're taking this too far."

"Trust me," he said. "I got you this far—right?" And I trusted him.

I was like the little brother Puffy never had. I had really good experiences with him. A lot of people said they had some negative experiences with him. But not me. I guess I was like an angel put in his presence. I never went through the stuff I would hear.

If we did have a problem, he'd know we had a problem. I would take it to him. If he did something I didn't like, I wouldn't show up for a show or taping. To me that was better than talk behind his back.

At this time we were doing a lot of publicity on his album, which featured me a lot. If he was acting up, I wouldn't show up to shows. One time we were supposed to go on *Soul Train* and something happened and I refused to go. He had to find somebody to do my part. But it wasn't the same.

People felt like I was only hurting myself. But I was actually getting my point across really quickly. If you don't stand for something you'll fall for anything, and I had to let him know that I was big on integrity. The money was nice, but I wasn't going to compromise on my integrity—I would rather just not show up.

That to me was handling it like a man. I didn't do a bunch of hollering and carrying on. I made my point and I was really clear. I guess that's why he respected me. Maybe that's what made him keep me around and work harder to make me a star—because he knew I was real with him, and I had his back, too.

He took good care of me. We had a level of respect that made it easier to gel and have chemistry. It got to the point where we were working so good together that we could read each other's mind. That's what made the music—the routines and everything we did—so powerful. We were operating in the same spirit, the same mind set with the same motivation, which was money. You rarely find people you can gel with like that, who can just click. We wanted to be the best.

In some people's mind I guess we were a little too close. And there were rumors about us. At first I didn't care. Me being a dude from the hood, I was just glad they were talking about me. Rumors were the last thing on my mind. I was trying to get that money. It didn't bother me. People judge you based on where their minds are.

But all the things that I saw and learned while I was in music only helps my ministry because I am aware of things. And nothing shocks me. I've been through it all and seen it all. Either I've seen it or I've done it. I've seen people love you that morning and can't stand you that afternoon. Wash the do-do out your drawers one day and the next day say they can't understand why they were ever with you in the first place. That same person who will promote you one day will demote you the next.

Everybody has a motive. I'm just trying to get everybody's motive to be heaven. God has done everything I thought couldn't be done. When I was living wrong I would believe anything because I was 100 percent obedient to the devil. Now I believe Christ because I want to be 100 percent obedient to Him.

The hardest thing for me in the beginning was when people would compare me to the other entertainers who came out of the world. But we ain't the same. No disrespect to any of them. I'm Pastor Mason Betha. Not Pastor Ma$e. Not Pastor M-A-$-E. Ma$e is of the devil. When you become a new creature, old things pass away and all things become new. Ma$e is the old thing. If you're done with the old thing, be done with it all the way.

If you were a stripper and you came to God, would you call yourself "Sister Caramel" or "Sister Peaches?" No. Because names are important. They have characteristics that go with them.

Many people come to God when things are going bad in their lives, and there's nothing wrong with that. But I came willingly to God while my career was still on top. And I was able to walk away from it all *with God's help*. What's the sacrifice if you come to the Lord after there is nothing left to give up?

I just want to see as many souls led to Christ as possible. And God can use many people to make that happen.

I even see Puff in God's plans. He has the potential. And I have a lot of love for him. I can't judge him. God called me over here to be able to bring people like Puff—and anyone else I can influence—out of that darkness. If I tried to be this political creature, I wouldn't be real. My job is to go get souls from the pit, who everyone thinks can't be saved and show them that they can live saved. I'm a living example of what God can do.

My life is on display to show people that you can give up everything and not lose a thing. If I didn't give up everything, how could I go back and tell them to do it? That's what makes the pull God has given me even more powerful. When I speak, it's the truth. My testimony eliminates all the excuses for why you can't surrender your life to the Lord.

There are a lot of people in my shoes; they just don't trust that they will be something without all of the money, the fame, the people around them. They have no faith. No faith in themselves. No faith in God. But still God is able!

Wherefore God gave them up to uncleanness, through the lusts of their own hearts, to dishonor their own bodies between themselves:

Who changed the truth of God into a lie, and worshipped and served the creature more than the Creator, who is blessed for ever. Amen.

—ROMANS 1:24-25

Sermon

*L*et's turn to Proverbs, chapter 27, verse 17 through 20.
The Bible says, Iron sharpeneth iron, so a man sharpeneth the countenance of his friends. Whoso keepeth the fig tree shall eat the fruit thereof. So he that waiteth on his master shall be honored. As water reflects a face, so the heart of man reflects the man. Hell and destruction are never full—so the eyes of men are never satisfied.

Y'all need me to read that again?

Keep your Bible right there. We're not going to go no further than that. We're just going to try to interpret this text.

The Bible says, "Iron sharpeneth iron." When I researched iron, I came up with a whole bunch of words. The one that stood out to me was strong. So the strong sharpeneth the strong.

To make it simpler, a Christian can sharpen another Christian. A young Christian can sharpeneth an old Christian and vice versa. A choir member can sharpeneth a minister. A deacon can sharpeneth a new believer. See, you can't get mad when God starts using other people because He gave you the choice first. You been going to church for the longest and you're scared to sing in the choir because you're afraid of what your friends might think.

All it's about is iron—iron sharpeneth iron. Which means that iron can sharpeneth copper but copper can't sharpeneth copper. What happens when iron is with copper? Copper is something that bends. You can meld it this way and when you want to bring it back this way you can bring it back another way, you can twirl it and spiral it. But iron doesn't bend. God is not calling us to be copper.

(sermon continued on page 67)

FOUR

Notoriety

I sat in the hotel room in Los Angeles, chilling with Mario—Super Mario—he was the A&R rep for Bad Boy at the time. We were waiting for people to get back from the Soul Train Music Awards and all the after-parties that followed.

On a normal night, I would have been at the Soul Train Music Awards. And on a normal night, I would have been at every after-party—dancing and finding girls to bring back to the hotel room. But something said, "Stay at the hotel."

It was about midnight, one o'clock, and I was half asleep after smoking a half a bag of weed on the couch in the suite at the Bel'Age Hotel.

"Yo, did y'all hear!" came this excited voice that had just bust through the door of the hotel room. "Biggie got shot! He might not make it!"

"What?!" There was nothing but disbelief and silence in that room. Me, Cooda, and Mario jumped into a car and rushed to the hospital. At the hospital folks were just lined up on the sidewalks and streets. It was a madhouse. There were people on cell phones telling people far away what had happened. "Biggie is dead, Yo, Biggie is dead!"

There were people sitting on the curb near the hospital with their heads in their hands. And there were people—a whole bunch of people—crying. Something very bad had happened.

"Yo, I can't do this no more!" I shouted. "I can't do this no more!"

Cooda grabbed me around the shoulders and tried to talk to me, "Yo, you gotta be strong," he said. But all I was thinking was, "I can't do this no more."

On a normal night, I would have been at that club with Biggie and Puff. On a normal night, I would have been in that black Chevy Suburban. On a normal night, I would have been in the seat closest to the door. On a normal night, I might have caught a bullet or two right along with Biggie. But this wasn't a normal night.

This was a night that began the change in the life of M-A-$-E.

I just got into this as a young dude. I didn't think there was going to be all the killing and the violence.

But right after Biggie was killed—when everyone was talking about Bad Boy crumbling, in the midst of all of the controversy, things got elevated to another level.

Biggie's death made my career in music larger. It made Puffy even bigger. Stuff just started flowing even better and we started making even more money. Biggie left a huge void and people were looking for something to fill it.

That's when *No Way Out* dropped and it slipped right in

that hole Biggie left. It was like Phil Jackson lost Jordan, and he slipped right over and found a new team to win a championship with.

Money was coming from everywhere. I'm doing a video with Chris Tucker, which was off the hook. "Feel So Good" was my first video for my own album. This video was hot. We had the best-looking women you could possibly meet. And access to the actual models made the video even hotter. One of the girls, Jazz, ended up becoming a tight friend of mine. But it was just a money-fest, a champagne-fest, a party-fest.

After that it was all over. Everything was like clockwork—flowing on schedule.

It's sad to say it but Biggie died for rap, but rap sure didn't die for Biggie. Christ is the only thing you should be dying for, because He's the only one who was willing to die for you. Dying for rap? That ain't the move.

That just shows you to be real careful what you put your faith in and what you say you're willing to die for—because of what you speak into creation happens. There is so much power in the tongue.

In the beginning, God said, "Let there be light." And there was. If we are made in God's image, we have the power to speak things into existence.

Biggie was talking about death and dying—*Life After Death* and *Ready to Die*. Tupac also rapped a lot about dying. He even said he couldn't see himself living long. He didn't.

Death is the one thing in life that's expected. But nobody thinks it can happen to them. I don't know a person who wakes up and says, "Today is it." People are scared to death of death. And I understand. When you are not with the Lord, death is real final. If you know you are not living right, you know where you're going. That's why people don't consider death.

Right now my mind set is, "Crash the plane!" I know where I'm going. "Bomb the building!" My Father has a room prepared for me.

When I was living on the streets, I, too, was afraid to die.

Biggie's death made me take life seriously. It was like, "He was just here!" and now he's gone. It scared me and made me work harder. Biggie in a lot of ways was my mentor. We used to talk about the business and best advice he gave me was, "Remember, it's just business. No matter how cool you become while doing business, it's just business."

And the LORD *said unto Moses, When thou goest to return into Egypt, see that thou do all those wonders before Phā´raōh, which I have put in their hand: but I will harden his heart that he shall not let the people go.*

—Exodus 4:21

Sermon

Water represents the Holy Spirit. When water sits too long on iron, it becomes rusty. Iron represents Christians. The iron not only becomes rusty, but once the iron becomes rusty, it is of no use no more. I can be iron, and let the Holy Spirit just sit on me—God's telling me to do some things—and I don't do them, then I become rusty. Now I never used to be iron. But when God made a little part of me iron, I never allowed the water to sit on me. When the water came through this iron—which was just a small pipe—I blew off steam. I never let the water just sit on me.

The Bible talks about The Word being a sword. The sword is a big piece of metal, a big piece of iron. There are many people who know a whole lot about The Word. You know the Bible from front to back and your sword is about ten feet long. However, you're not cutting anybody with the truth of The Word because your sword is not sharp anymore. You're not hanging around people who are sharp, meaning people who live by The Word. When you cut—spread God's message—it takes you twenty conversations to help someone make up their mind that they want to be saved.

God has called us to be iron—strong men of God, strong women of God. He hasn't called us to be weak men of God, weak women of

God, weak kids of God, weak boys of God, weak girls of God. See me, I'm just a person—like I said, I'm a small piece of iron. I'm just a razor, but if I get the right artery I can make something happen with this small piece of iron—just a small piece. If you're swinging a rusty sword with no sharpness to it, and I'm swinging that little Gillette razor, I'm still more powerful. I don't know the whole Bible. I haven't finished reading the whole Bible. But the little part I know is sharp. I'm doing a lot with that little razor. He never said how big the iron had to be, He just said that the iron sharpeneth iron.

(sermon continued on page 83)

Let My People Go!

I was in a hotel with Khalilah. She was this person I went to school with at Manhattan Center and I got her a job working for Bad Boy handling publicity. I told her, "I'm out!" I asked her if she could make a call to Hot 97—which is the biggest hip-hop station in New York City, where I knew I would have the biggest audience. I wanted to make my decision publicly to show God I wasn't ashamed.

"Are you sure? If you do this now, there's no turning back," she said.

"If I wait, I'm never going to do it," I said.

You know how people say, "I'm going to do it tomorrow," and tomorrow something comes up. And then the next day, something else happens. Before you know it tomorrow never comes.

Khalilah called Hot 97, it was a little after four o'clock—a time when plenty of people would be listening. Bugsy, the deejay during that time, answered. We had a direct line into the studio. I took the phone and told Bugsy what I wanted to do. I told him I was leaving the music business and I wanted to announce it on his show.

"Man, I know you're just going through some stuff," Bugsy said. "But I want you to think about what you're saying because you sound a little hasty. And this is a big decision. If you call back I'll let you say whatever you want. But I want you to think about it first."

He must of thought I was playing. Nobody wanted to believe me. Or they wanted to believe I was crazy or tripping. But I wasn't. I took his advice and thought about it. And I prayed, "God, let your will be done." I had Khalilah call back around six o'clock and it seemed like it took forever for somebody to pick up the line. While it was still ringing I said, "God, if you don't want me to do this, don't let them pick up the phone."

Funkmaster Flex picked up the phone. It was April 4, 1999. I will never forget the date. Flex picked up the phone and I said, "Yo, this is Ma$e!" And I told him what I was about to do. He put me on the air and I said, "I called the radio station to let you know I thank you for all the support you've given me in the past. And I'm out this piece. Y'all are so caught up in this game, you can't even see it. Maybe later on y'all will understand. I'm out. I have to follow God."

A few hours later I hooked up with Foxy Brown. She and I had become friends, especially after I found out that her brother, Gavin, and I used to play basketball at Riverside Church. She used to try to beat me up all the time—try to provoke me to see if she could get me worked up. She thought it was so funny that I was always so cool. Foxy was like my little sister and I had talked to her about what I was planning on doing before I actually did it.

She said, "If you do it, I will do it, too!"

We used to always talk about how fickle the business was.

I asked her, "Out of all the money we had, is it worth it?"

She would say, "No. If I can get this money some other way, I'd do it."

That was the way a lot of people in the business felt. They may not have said those words, but their eyes said it all. Everybody loves the money you make, but why is everybody so unhappy?

They think cars and jewelry make up for everything you don't have. See, people watch all of that on TV. They see the videos and they see how these rappers are living and they think, "They have everything." But they don't have peace within themselves. No Bentley, no jewelry, no woman can give you that peace. That's why they smoke a lot because they're looking for peace. But that's fake peace. That's why they drink so much. That's why they party so much.

They're looking for something or somebody to make them feel the way they want to feel inside but can't. I know Foxy wanted that peace, too.

I hooked up with her at my favorite restaurant in New York—the Shark Bar. I met her outside and we were just hanging out on Amsterdam Avenue in front of the Shark Bar.

"Yo, I did it," I said. "I quit."

She just stared at me and finally said, "What?!" She couldn't believe that I actually did it. She remembered what she said about doing it too, but the devil changed her mind. He came in there with doubt. And pride. "What if this doesn't work?" she said. But God doesn't work in "what ifs." He's a certain God.

"God is telling you to leave, too, for a reason," I said.

"Yeah, I'm a do it," she said. "But I got to do it in my own time."

While Foxy and I were outside the Shark Bar talking, a car pulls up. Pharaoh showed up. In the book of Exodus, Moses was trying to show Pharaoh that he had to let the children of Israel go or else bad things would happen to the kingdom of Egypt. Moses and Pharaoh were brothers. There was a lot of love between them. But when Moses left and came back with that message from God, Pharaoh's heart became hard.

It was the same way on that night in front of the Shark Bar when I had to face Pharaoh. He didn't want to let the people go.

He said, "What's wrong?" But he knew. He heard I was leaving.

"Nothing is wrong," I said. "This is just something I have to do."

And I guess—it is my assumption—that Pharaoh must have thought at the time that it was a money issue for me. So he called in Senior Pharaoh, the head of Arista Records. I went up to the Arista office and Senior Pharaoh said, "Did God or man tell you to do this?"

I said, "I have to leave."

"You need to think about what you're going to do," Senior Pharaoh said. "How are you going to pay your bills? You have a lifestyle now and everything we told you we would do, we did it. You're just going to upset a lot of people and you're playing with people's money."

He even tried to hit me with this: "Hey, even in church, they need money. Even if you're going to go to church you need money."

"No," I said. "My God will supply my needs."

Then he told me if I broke my contract, "We're not obligated to give you any money from your album."

He was testing me to see if I was serious. At first I paused and thought about it. I excused myself and went to the bathroom down the hall. I got on my knees and prayed. God was speaking with me, "How can you think so supernaturally and then when they talk about money you think so naturally?" I knew I had to do what God told me.

I went back into the room and told them, "If I don't get any money from my album, that's fine because I'm finished." Pharaoh ended up making sure that I got the rest of the money, which was surprising because it showed me a different side of him.

He understood that leaving was something I had to do as a man. Me and Pharaoh were always cool. He didn't take my decision personally. In fact, once he realized I was serious, he was more supportive than anybody else.

But I call him Pharaoh because in the Bible, Pharaoh and Moses were cool until Moses came back and told him to let the people go. I told Pharaoh to let the people go. I told him even if he didn't feel *he* could leave, he had to let other people go.

In the process of me telling him to let the people go, I realized that some of the people didn't want to be free, they were happy living in Egypt. They were happy smoking and drinking. They thought they were happy living that lifestyle.

There were some who did want to be free. So what I was telling Pharaoh was out of the best interest for him as well.

God wanted to get his attention. Pharaoh is a leader. In the Bible, God went after the leaders knowing that if they sold out for Him they would bring so many souls with them. You get the head, and the followers will follow.

After telling me what I needed to do in walking away from the music business, my second vision was about Pharaoh. God was removing all these people from him to get his attention.

There was Craig Mack. The Lox. Tonya Blount. Me. And some others. With each person, there were many more people's lives affected. Pharaoh's decisions didn't just affect him and his artists. Around each artist is a road manager, a marketing person, an A&R person, a publicist, etc. Then there are at least five family members on top of that. And that doesn't include the seven-man entourage.

Then you have to look at the tragedies. The people who died at City College. There was Biggie. And Shyne, who was sentenced to some years in prison. There was also a little boy who flipped out at a photo shoot. He took off all of his clothes and started masturbating right there at the shoot. He was like twelve years old. He just flipped out. That's crazy. You can't stay around the devil's work and say it won't affect you. You can't lay in pig's slop and think you're clean.

Seeing all of this, knowing all of this—how can you stay?

I pray for all the Pharaohs out there. I'm not sure if they're going to listen. The Pharaoh I knew didn't. But I stay patient because God was patient with me.

It becomes deceitful because for the right price even some carnal saints will tell you keep it up, you are still God's child. And that's cool. But I just ask, which God? Your God is whatever you worship. Money can be your God.

You can say "God" as much as you want. You can say you're spiritual. Which spirit? There is the spirit of lust. There is the spirit of deceit. You can say you're religious. But you put your pants on religiously. I hope you brush your teeth religiously.

The Bible says you will know the tree by its fruits and for us to be ye separate. There has to be some distinction between the world and God. It don't seem like a lot of people are about God these days. It seems like it's about money.

If it's about God, then there will be some evidence of that. If it's about money, that too will show. There are a lot of artists—a lot of people in general—who walk around talking about God, but keep doing evil to people with no remorse. That's a contradiction. There are many who say, "Lord, Lord," but where is the evidence of their relationship? I'm not judging. I'm just raising some questions and speaking the truth. If you know a tree by its fruits, I'm just fruit inspecting.

There are many who do things for charity or think they can throw money at God and not have to own up to their own sin. If it's not about God, all the riches in the world you try to give a church or a charity is in vain. If you don't give God your heart, it's in vain. Before we offer God money, we have to offer him our heart, our soul.

Are you Holy Ghost–filled? Are you fire-baptized? Is the spirit working in you? You'll know by the fruits. Bitter water don't come from a sweet fountain. It wouldn't be right to praise God and curse God out of the same mouth. You see people talking about, "I got all these girls, and all this money." Then when they win an award they say, "The Lord gave me this." That wasn't the Lord. That's a contradiction.

I challenge those who are entertaining to keep it real. In no way do I want to discourage them. But I can't tell them a lie because that's what they want to hear. They think by doing gospel, they are doing God's work. They think they are helping God win souls.

Who are we to say we can help God? Just think about it. There is nowhere in the Bible that it says God needs us to help Him. He's omnipotent—all-powerful. The Word says he's omnipresent, which means he's everywhere. Where can we go, where God is not? He's omniscient. All-knowing. What do we know that He doesn't know?

Sometimes we err in trying to help God. I don't run around trying to help God. God's going to do what God's going to do. I could be hounding every artist I know to do what I'm doing. God didn't send me to hound them yet. First, he's getting my testimony all the way together.

I don't believe my testimony is finished. I know when I speak to people, I'm going to have to show them something. I don't have anything to prove. But when God sends me back to them, it will be something great.

I don't want to go on Mason's power and Mason's strength. I want to go as a totally changed man, with the evidence of what God can do. The only reason I didn't return right after making my decision to turn my life over to God was because I knew that those people were stronger in the devil than I was in Christ.

It would be like pulling in a shark with a fish hook—the chances of you getting that shark out of that water are slim. However that shark could have pulled me back into the water with him and killed me. That's why God has given me these years to build myself and build my faith. When we go get those entertainers, someone's coming home—the Lord is bringing them home for sure. I thank God for the opportunity to help, because even though God don't need me, He will use me.

I couldn't see myself rapping again, not even to do gospel. That would be crazy. I know I still have an ear for music and maybe God will use it for something. But I can't see myself rapping. I don't even want to be talking over some music with people doing all the singing and I'm making all the money. You know that's crazy. I don't knock those who do it. That's on them, whatever floats their boat.

Some people get converted and they don't want nothing else but to please God. They love the way it feels to please Christ so much that they don't want to mess that up. That's where I am. There are other people who feel they can be saved and yet still do what they used to do—like music. So instead of doing secular, they switch to gospel with the same secular feel. It ain't for me to judge whether that's wrong. I'm just saying if what I do might possibly lead some people astray, why even do it?

Rather than do something that's controversial that will lead some people to heaven and end up leading more people to hell, I would rather just leave behind what I used to do altogether. Now, when Judgment Day comes and the Lord says, "What you did led some of my people to hell,"? All the fame and money in the world would not have been worth it, now would it?

The Bible even states: Stay away from the appearance of evil. If it don't look right, nine times out of ten, it's probably not right.

I think we're in a time when no one wants to be responsible. Those who try to stand for something—they're the ones who look crazy. I feel in order for you to be an owner, you must take ownership, take responsibility for things, even for those who are not responsible. If somebody throws garbage in your yard, do you leave it there? You didn't do it, but you pick it up because it's your yard.

I came out of music—I'm taking ownership of that music. I must own up to what's wrong with it. I have to be responsible for people who don't want to be responsible.

Now, it would take a person who has been in rap and with Christ to know what kind of music is not of Christ. Sometimes I just have to break it down for people to understand where I'm coming from. There is gospel R&B. R&B is rhythm and blues. Does God produce blues? There is gospel jazz. Jazz is mixed-up melodies put together to sound sweet and harmonious. I guess you're saying that God is the author of confusion? The best rap music is the most arrogant, with the most demonic message. How can you mix it with God?

In the book of Revelation, God says that we are not to add nothing to His word, or take anything away. People say they want to reach young people so they have to use music that young people want to listen to. What happens when young people want to listen to pimps? Do we make gospel pimps? You're trying to change God to fit what the people want. What got you saved? The Bible says God doesn't change.

You can't force somebody into loving Christ as a choice.

I know what Paul did to win over the Gentiles. But who are you following, Paul or Jesus? Jesus didn't have to rap to get people saved. Jesus didn't convert Christianity into R&B to get people saved. We are following Jesus, right?

I got a lot of criticism for what I did because what God helped me to do wasn't common. I was criticized everywhere. And it became real stressful.

The entertainment world didn't want to accept it and the people in the church didn't want to receive me in the beginning. Today, I'm considered a blessing to any congregation because of what God is doing with me.

At first people were questioning why I really left and that led to people saying all types of foolishness out of their mouths. I was even compared to David Koresh when I was holding Bible study on the campus of Clark University in Atlanta because the students were changing dramatically for the better.

But the more they tried to destroy my name, the more I knew I was pleasing God. When I start telling the truth, I don't want them to think I'm judging. I'm not assuming what they're doing is wrong. I'm just telling the facts. Judging is saying something based on someone else's evidence. I'm talking about things I know, because I've been there.

And what I know is there are a lot of unhappy souls in entertainment and throughout the world. There are a lot of people in bondage who are too afraid to do what it will take to bring peace into their lives. There are a lot of people who know better who are holding onto artists because of their greed and their fear. Most of them grew up in church or have a strong church background.

The only reason for me speaking or writing is for God to use me to get their attention.

Now faith is the substance of things hoped for, the evidence of things not seen.

—HEBREWS 11:1

Sermon

*T**he Bible says,* The iron sharpeneth the iron, so a man sharpeneth the countenance of his friends. *Sharpens the countenance of his friends. You mean to tell me I'm accountable for my friends? You mean to tell me God is going to judge me by the people I'm hanging around? You mean to tell me that God is not pleased with the people I'm hanging around? Now I'm going to tell you something about the countenance of your friend. What is your friend? What is the countenance?*

A friend is somebody who, when everything goes wrong, is there. We don't have a lot of friends. We have a lot of acquaintances.

Now let's deal with the countenance of the friend. If my pastor's friend is hanging around with me and I'm no good for him, then he's accountable for hanging around me. When I first came to God and all my ways weren't right, I wasn't mad that my pastor wasn't hanging around me, as I was still doing some things I knew weren't right. As a friend, I had to respect his decision. Initially, I wasn't ready to give my life totally to God. I knew I would eventually get there, but as a friend, I couldn't slow anybody up in terms of where God is trying to take them.

The Bible says, So a man sharpeneth the countenance of his friends. *Sharpeneth. People claim to be around their wayward* friends in an attempt to save them. *How else are they going to get saved? Jesus was around the sinners.*

A man sharpeneth the countenance of his friends. *Which means, I'm trying to sharpen the man who's not saved. If he doesn't intend to get sharp, he has to get cut off.*

A man sharpeneth the countenance of his friends.

Let's talk about "getting cut off." When a snake is poisonous, you need to get poison away by cutting its head off. Now if I'm hanging around people, who aren't sharp, then they're like snakes. If you hang around snakes, eventually you will get bitten. And once you get bitten, you're poisoned. Once you become poisoned you can die. My old friends could be compared to snakes because they aren't really ready to give their lives to God. They are not ready to take this journey with me.

(sermon continued on page 101)

SIX

My Job Is Working for Jesus

I got on an afternoon flight to Atlanta from JFK. My boy, Hud, was driving my Mercedes down to Atlanta to meet me. He left earlier that day. Dale, my bodyguard, my homie, drove my Range Rover.

I was on the plane, in first class, sipping orange juice and just not feeling right. I felt like I was leaving something behind. I wanted to go up and tell the pilot to turn the plane around because I had to go back. Something wasn't right. I had to go back.

That was my flesh talking, saying, "You can't leave all that money behind. They're gonna give you millions if you go back. You're just about to be what you always thought you'd become."

Nah! Where I was going, what I was about to do, was going to save my life.

On my way home, I felt like I was driving home with a bride and we were newlyweds.

But when I stepped through the door of my house, I started feeling that feeling again. I didn't feel right in my own place. The weed was still on the counter in a jar where I kept it, like sugar. The box of cigars was there, too, even though I had quit using cigars to roll my weed ever since I heard that cigars give you cancer quicker than regular paper.

The condoms were still in the drawers, all over the house. I had them everywhere just in case. I never knew where I might end up with a girl or girls in that house so I had to be covered. Everything was just where I left it. But something wasn't right.

I wasn't right, according to the voice of the devil.

I sat on Ma$e's couch with my hands on my head and my elbows on my knees and I started looking at all Ma$e possessed. His system was one of the phattest Sony systems they made. And all my CDs and DATs—the masters that you put your music on for concerts—were lined up all neatly in the room.

I got up and started cracking every disc, breaking them in half, stomping on them. All my plaques and awards—all the things Ma$e won—I threw in a pile in the middle of the room. I scooped up the mess in bags and I threw it out. I had to get them out of the house—away from me. It took days to get all of that stuff out of the house, and when I was finished, I sat on the floor against the wall—I got rid of the couch, too—and I felt better. I sat there thinking, "I'm free!"

Every man gets a moment to come to himself, whether he wants to do it or not, and make that move. You have to have a moment where you ask yourself, "What am I doing?" and "Where am I going?" But I had to ask this question: "Who am I?"

Before this day, I was Ma$e. A guy who lived for the moment, where tomorrow didn't even matter. The old Ma$e was six feet, brown skin, a hundred and ninety pounds and diamonds was his first name. He felt like the Earth was in his hands. Out of his mouth came doctrine. If he said it, the people lived it. If he wrote it, the people bought it. If he drove it, the people leased it.

Ma$e revolutionized rap. He changed the whole hip-hop world. He was the reason why everyone wore shiny jean suits. He started it, now it's the style. He's the reason they put down Versace and got into sportswear. He came in with a whole new feel—baseball jerseys, football jerseys—stuff nobody was really wearing in the industry before. Waves and wave caps. That was Ma$e.

Ma$e was a jerk who didn't follow anybody's rules. Whatever way they told him to act, he would do the opposite.

One time he was at BET just after Puff's *No Way Out* album had dropped. He was supposed to be interviewed by Rachel. Before they went out on the stage, they told Ma$e that Rachel was married to one of the producers, she was very nice and that he should be nice to her. They knew Ma$e. And I guess by them telling him she was nice and married to one of the producers would stop him from acting up. Wrong!

Don't you know, Ma$e went out and started flirting with her on live TV. He asked her if she had a man. She said yes. And he said, "Who's faithful these days?" And he was serious. That was Ma$e. Ma$e could have anything he wanted! I would meet girls who went to church and I could get them to sleep with me or whatever I wanted. That would be a thing to show God. It was the same thing Satan did—tried to show God that he was in control. I was of the devil at one time.

It's scary when you realize where you've been. And half the people who are there now don't even know it. They don't even know they're working for Satan.

As Ma$e, I was working for him so long I thought this was the way life was supposed to be. I thought life was all about money, women, and having a good time.

"You only live once," I thought. And if you don't plan on going to heaven, you're absolutely right—you do only live once. People in general live like there ain't no tomorrow because they don't plan on living like there's a tomorrow.

I planned on living. I wanted what God had for me. I knew I had to quit my old job because God had a new one for me. And it started with being a new person.

After throwing away all the things that used to be important to me, the things that made me Ma$e, especially music— I could breathe. I sat on the kitchen counter, and my heart was beating as calm as possible. I said to myself, "I don't know what I just started here, but I like the way it feels." I wouldn't trade it for anything.

And how I was feeling inside must have been showing on the outside because people were acting funny toward me. No matter where I went, I would get these funny looks. I would go to the mall (I still love to shop) and people wouldn't know what to do or say. I would be in Lenox Mall or Phipps Mall, Cumberland Mall, Northlake or Southlake Mall, wherever I went, people would look at me like I was a ghost. It was like they were scared to speak.

They had heard I left the music industry for God and they didn't know whether they should say, "Whattup, my nigga!"

like they used to do when I was Ma$e, or "Hallelujah" or "Bless you" and keep walking.

So for a couple of months it seemed like nobody was speaking to me at all. I would go to my gym, Crunch in Buckhead, and people weren't saying anything to me at all. Now they speak to me. But at first they were like, "This dude is crazy."

There were those who were into God, though. And they would let me know that I was all right. They would say, "I really respect what you did." Or they would come up to me—always at the right time, when I was feeling bad or low—and say, "Stay strong!" or "It takes a man to do what you did." Thank you. That encouragement would keep me going.

It was hard at first. It was hard to give up the life I lived. But my Spirit Man wouldn't let that life live anymore.

When my boys Hud and Dale showed up with my cars, I didn't even want to drive them anymore. And before, I loved my cars. But every time I would drive one of them, I didn't feel right. So I started letting other people drive them. So I knew I had to give them away—if I didn't, I felt like I was blocking what God had in store for me.

And on Sunday, it was confirmed in church. The pastor was preaching his sermon and he said, "You wondering why God's not moving in your life? There's sin in the camp. God don't move when there's sin in the camp."

He was preaching from the book of Joshua, talking about Achan and the people with Joshua had brought back unclean things to the camp and tried to hide it. And for that reason God didn't give them victory. I went home and prayed. And God showed me that I had unclean things in my camp. I didn't want nothing to block God from doing what he said he was going to do for me. I had to put myself in the position to be blessed.

I had to get rid of all that stuff because it reminded me of Ma$e. No matter how holy I felt. No matter how much in the spirit I was. No matter how close I was getting to God, the things I had—the cars, the house, the jewelry, everything came from me serving the devil—they were unclean to me. I could have cast the demonic spirits off and prayed over the cars, the jewelry, the house. But the only way I could be certain that I was doing right was to get rid of them all together.

Cars and jewelry represented wealth and good living to Ma$e. They were status symbols that let people know Ma$e was a baller, that he was a major player in the game. Today cars only represent transportation.

The jewelry was about getting the looks. It represented two stares instead of one. It reminded people that Ma$e was in a room. Today I only wear a bracelet made of rubber that I got from my pastor that says "Fear Not" with a cross on it. And I wear a watch to tell time, not to impress people.

And the only other jewelry I'm going to add will be my wedding band. I'm glad I took off all of the diamonds and platinum. It makes me feel good to know that the jewels don't make me. I hear people say all the time, "Yeah, it don't make me either, I just like it." And that's cool. But for me, I'm done with it. I'm done with that phase of my life.

When I was Ma$e I allowed myself to be dragged into those areas where vanity ruled me. I only wanted things because I cared what people thought. Now I only care what God thinks. There was a time when I thought if I didn't have a whole bunch of jewelry and cars and material things, that I was nothing. I know now that Jesus made me and that makes me something.

Wearing jewelry and buying nice cars won't necessarily send you to hell. But if you put those things before God, it will. I knew I had a weakness in that area. Why leave a question? I'd rather be sure. Some things I don't know about, whether they're right or wrong. But when it comes to going to heaven, I'm not leaving it up to chance or maybe. If there's even a question, I have to get rid of it.

So I got the keys and title to my car and I drove it to the church. I didn't tell anybody what I was going to do. I just had to do it. When I got to the church, I handed the title and the keys to one of the members. They were in shock, they couldn't believe it. They said they couldn't accept it and tried to give me back the keys. But I said, "God wants you to have this." I told them not to tell a soul that I gave it to them. I wanted them to say that God did it. Because God did do it.

There is no way I would have given away a Mercedes unless God told me to. I would never have done it on my own, so they had to give God the glory. I felt so good, so free after doing it.

But I wasn't completely obedient, and I paid for it. You know you can't halfway serve God. Once you put your foot in that water, you have to jump in—whole body. If you don't, God will have a way of pulling you in.

I decided I would try to keep the Range Rover. I figured I had done enough giving away the Mercedes. If I gave up this one, I would be without a car and I didn't think God wanted me to be totally without a car. Little did I know.

But when He says give up everything, He means *everything*.

A couple a nights a week, I would play ball at this gym called the Run N Shoot in Atlanta. I parked the Jeep where I always did out back, went into the gym and exchanged my car keys for a locker key—just as I had done for months. When I was finished playing, I would give them their key back and get my car keys and go home. But when I went to return the locker key this time, the lady at the desk said she couldn't find my keys.

I knew something was up then. I couldn't even be too upset, because I knew. I went outside and the Range Rover was gone. There was an empty space where I parked it. I kept hearing God's words, "Give away everything," and I couldn't be mad. I was disobedient.

I went back into the gym and called the police. They found it pretty quickly. But everything in it was gone—including my system, my wallet, everything. And even worse, I had taken off all my jewelry before I went into the gym and put it behind the front seat. It was all gone, too. There was a chain, some diamond earrings and this amazing diamond ring Puff had bought me. All of it was gone. Even my Bible. The pastor's wife had given me a study Bible that I brought everywhere with me. They took that too.

When I got back into the gym, the lady—the who said she couldn't find my keys—was gone. I knew she had something to do with it. I just hope she got something out of it, and does something good with whatever she got.

They later found the Jeep at the bottom of a hill, crashed against a pole. Whoever took it parked it at the top of the hill, put it in neutral, pushed it down the hill into a pole. This let me know it was personal. They could have kept it or stripped it for the money. It's like when a guy gets shot in the head ten times—that's personal.

The Jeep was only damaged on one side. But I got it fixed and gave it away.

And within a Sunday after giving the Range Rover away, someone had returned my Bible to the church. Besides getting the actual Jeep back, that Bible was the only thing that was returned intact. That was amazing. God was showing me that His word is all I need.

If I follow His word, I will get back everything. I will get another car. I will get another house. His word held the key. And people will know that it is Him who is doing it.

The Lord has found favor. He touched other people's hearts to be a huge blessing. Just to show me He got me. It feels good to know that God is loving you. How much better can it be to know God loves you? If God's feeling you, who else you need to feel you? That's the best feeling in the world.

It's nice to walk past a bunch of women and they are looking at you and, say to yourself, "Yeah, they feeling me." You know how that feels. How much better does it feel to have God feeling you? How good does it feel that the one who built this Earth, the God of this universe, is in love with you? That's the greatest feeling. It feels better than being high, than having your best whatever. It makes you want to scream where there's nothing scaring you. It makes you want to jump with joy. It's unexplainable.

I used to hear old men in church talk about the joy of the Lord and I couldn't understand it. But I do now. It makes you cry and ain't nobody bothering you. It makes you run and ain't nobody chasing you. It makes you have an outbreak and people look at you like you're crazy. The joy is so deep, it makes people look at you and they want what you've got. "Whatever he's on, that's what I need a bag of," they think. "Whatever he's drinking, that's what I want to drink!"

But what I'm on is Jesus. And, yes, you too, can experience it if you want to. But with that feeling comes a sacrifice. I had to give up everything to gain joy. And even with that joy come some trials, comes some sadness—things that make you want to run in the opposite direction.

Just when I started seeing God work in my life, it was like the enemy was coming after me even harder just to discourage me about the decision I made.

It was pulling up to a year since I left music and turned my life over to the Lord. I spent every day studying the Bible or going to church or visiting a church or going on a mission with my pastor somewhere in the country woods. I wasn't worried about nothing but serving the Lord. I wasn't even worried about how I looked. I let my hair grow and I had an afro. I even let my body go and stopped working out. I was getting skinny again the way I was in high school. I let everything go.

My accountant called me from New York and told me that I had enough money to live on, but I had to start to generate some kind of income soon because that money was getting real low. He told me to consider getting a job or doing something.

Ever since that day I broke up all those CDs, I was totally turned off to rap, hip-hop, and even R&B music. I no longer listened to that kind of music, even on the radio. I stopped watching music videos. And I don't even let people who visit turn to those stations.

Once you know what it's like being on crack, you can't even be around someone who smells like it. You can't stop smoking crack and keep your stem around for old memories. A person can disagree with me. But I would ask you to go without watching rap videos or listening to that music on the radio for a week. And I want you to tell me the difference in your life in just one week. I guarantee there will be a difference. Is your conscience clearer? How different are the decisions you make?

I only listen to gospel—mostly the old-style gospel from back in the day. I was listening to this gospel station while driving in my car and this song came on by Darius Twyman. He was singing about a job he had working for Jesus—all through the night and all through the day. That was so funny to me that it became my favorite song.

When my accountant started talking to me about finding a job, I began singing to him, "My job is working for Jesus. All through the night and all through the day."

I had offers to do a whole bunch of stuff. I could have spoken at a whole bunch of places for lots of money. But I wasn't ready for God to speak through me. My life wasn't together yet. I wasn't where I needed to be and I couldn't stand up in front of people lying. They say the spirit knows the spirit and people would know that my spirit was still not right. Then there were people wanting me to do stuff as Ma$e. But I had to tell them, "I'm not him no more."

I had to keep working for Jesus until I learned how to do my job well. My accountant left me alone. But I got my first taste of reality, my first test of faith, less than a month after our little talk. I had to go somewhere with my pastor and I ran home to change my clothes. I walked through the door and went to flick on the lights and nothing happened. My electricity had been turned off.

"My lights ain't on?!" I said to myself.

I couldn't believe it. No matter where I lived, no matter how little money we had growing up, my lights had never been turned off. The long distance on my phone was shut down too. I discovered this when I tried to call my accountant in New York to see what was up. I was so upset. I was at a low point. Never in my life had I experienced this. And I thought that by giving away everything that I was going to be rewarded. I thought I would get it all back immediately. But you can't look for God to work on your timetable. He works in His own time.

It had been nearly eight months since I gave away all my clothes, lost or gave away all my jewelry, gave away the cars. What else was there? Then the words people were saying started coming into my mind.

"You put up a good fight," they would say. "There is no shame in going back now." I would hear, "You made your point, you can go back." And these were people close to me, people who I thought loved me who were saying these things. Even church folks would say, "Nobody expects you to go this route all the way. You're an entertainer. Go back."

But the more those words started rolling off their tongues, the more determined I became. It gave me fuel. Before I quit, I'll add more to my testimony. Before I give up, I'll make sure more people get saved.

As I stood there in the dark, with no one to call, I made a decision—I'm never going back. God wanted to show me I could do this—with no lights, no telephone, no cars, no jewelry, no people. All I needed was Him.

I went to church that Sunday and started praising God like I ain't never praised God before. I was crying and praising Him. "Glory to Your name!" People saw me and many didn't know what I was going through. And they saw me and said, "How is he so weary, yet praising God like that?" Once that got into people's spirit, they rallied around me so much. Siloam Baptist Church knew I was being tested and they stuck by me.

They knew the devil was coming after me. The enemy was screaming at me, "You're going to speak against me? After all I've done for you, you're going to go against me? Well, all right, I'm going to show you!"

But that just gave me more fuel.

When I went home the next evening, everything was back on. When I left the day before, everything was off. But when I came home, my electricity was back on and so was the phone. Somebody paid my bills. I don't know who in the physical. And ever since that day, somehow, some way, all my bills have been paid.

God told me to keep His word in my heart and live like I don't want for nothing. And I did. And now it's like all types of miracles come my way—just for doing God's work. And in no way, shape, form, or fashion do I compromise the words God has given me. I do it just the way he tells me to do it. And everything comes my way. Every single thing.

I don't have a conventional job. I have a job working for Jesus. Whatever is right, he'll pay. All I got to do is make sure that I'm right and He's going to pay for everything.

My pastor used to say to me, "Boy, you know what? You

got that old-school religion faith. Wherever you go, keep that."

Old-school religion faith is faith the way God says it, where you just believe what He tells you without question, without explanation. You wait on Him and, even if it sounds crazy, you do it. Nowadays, people only believe what they can see or what makes sense to them. That ain't faith.

Faith is the substance of things hoped for and the evidence of things not seen.

I got that kind of faith. I believe that God can do anything. If I didn't believe it I would have gone back. There were many days I struggled. There were many days I could have gone back.

But I said, "No, Satan! Before I give up my testimony, I'm going to add more to it!" With me holding on, it's just going to make more people come to the kingdom. I told him, "You better find someone else to play with!"

If the devil can ruin you, he can ruin someone else's faith too. But if you hold on, somebody else will have an opportunity to come to the kingdom . . . and the devil loses. That's the chance Satan takes messing with a faithful saint. If he can make a faithful saint fall, a bunch of people fall, too. But if the saint can hold on and be victorious, a bunch of people will come to the Lord. That's how it works. And once I understood that fight—that we're in a war for souls—I couldn't even think about looking back to what I had, to what I was.

Beware of false prophets, which come to you in sheep's clothing, but inwardly they are ravening wolves.

Ye shall know them by their fruits. Do men gather grapes of thorns, or figs of thistles?

—MATTHEW 7:15-16

Sermon

*S*o *we went over,* iron sharpeneth iron so the man
sharpeneth the countenance of his friends. *In the next
Scripture, which is a significant piece in "hell is never full," there
are four important words, which I'll break down so everybody can
understand the entire meaning of this passage. It says,* Whoso
keepeth the fig tree shall eat the fruit thereof. So he that
waiteth on his master shall be honored.

*It says "whoso"—not Ma$e. Whoso—not the First Baptist
Church, but whoso. The man who's on TV every day—is whoso.
The old man who has been preaching for 48 years—is whoso. The
little kid whose father is a pastor—is whoso. That means the guy
who's a backslider. The guy who's in jail and wants to change is
whoso. The guy who wants to quit rapping to give his life to God is
whoso. The guy who used to sell drugs is whoso. Y'all get where I'm
going with this whoso?*

The next phrase reads whoso keepeth the fig tree. *When I
researched fig tree, it says, "A fig tree gets paid for its pain." For
quite some time I contemplated how a fig tree could get paid for its
pain. There are two ways a fig tree can get paid for its pain. A fig
tree grows upright because it stands by itself. It is also sturdy and
unshakable because of its strong roots. See, a lot of people don't want*

to stand as a fig tree—alone and strong. A fig tree has a whole bunch of branches and looks like it has nothing else. What branches got to do with me? People say, I do a whole lot of studying but I have nothing. I go to church every Sunday, but I have nothing. I read the word, I study the word, I'm on fire. But I look like I have nothing. But the Bible says, "He that keepeth the fig tree shall eat the fruit thereof."

You got people who are fig trees right now. And think about when a fig tree is by itself. That's where you see the crow. The crow only comes around when (the fig tree) is by itself. You never see a crow on a flourishing tree. He's always on a fig tree.

(sermon continued on page 111)

SEVEN

False Prophets

Being a prophet is not much different than being a rapper. They're just serving a different master. In rap, you serve the devil and the money, and things are your God. Today I am serving God Almighty and my only destination is heaven for myself and everyone else I can reach.

Rap is Running Away from Preaching. Those who are really dominant in rap all have a way with words. But they're using their words for the wrong things. To be a rapper you have to be able to speak in parables well. That's the way Jesus spoke. You have to be a quick thinker—able to respond to questions and answer critics on the spot. That's what Jesus did. A rapper is one who carries a message. He's a prophet even if he doesn't want to be a prophet. He speaks the word and the people carry it out. That's what Jesus did. They say, "This is how you dress." And the people dress that way. "This is what you should be driving," and the people break their necks and wallets to get those cars.

Sad to say, rap is a doctrine. They say what they believe and it's embedded in the minds of young people, and they follow it. Rappers are prophets who are used by the devil and most of them don't realize it. Either that or they don't want to come to grips with the trip.

I used to be onstage talking about "God bless," and walk off and smoke a blunt. Or give praises to God at award shows and then have five girls waiting in the hotel room. God knows my heart—that's what everyone says. God also knows when our mouth is close but our heart is far from Him.

Your God and your Lord is whoever you work for. If money owns you—that's your God. If that's what you live for—that's your God. I have a problem with people using Jesus' and God's name in vain. If you want to keep doing what you're doing, do it. But don't put it in God's name.

Why are we here? To make it into heaven, to make it down that narrow road and get inside those pearly gates. We're not here for anything else.

The Scripture says only the righteous will see God. If people produce certain kinds of music and they think it's righteous, more power to them. But if what they're doing leads even one person to hell, woe unto them.

I want to sit down and talk to the top rappers and singers in the game. But they duck and dodge me. The people around them keep us from conversing. When I go to New York, everyone is ghost—nowhere to be found. And I understand. You think an A&R person wants me to have a one-on-one with DMX? Does a record company CEO want me to have an afternoon brunch with Jay-Z or Lauren Hill? That's their biggest fear. Because once they get the knowledge they will run with it. And where will that leave the rap business? I'm a cancer to what they're doing. You think people like putting my calls through when I call Bad Boy? I'm an enemy of the state.

I could possibly get killed for that. I'm messing with millions, no, *billions* of dollars. But I know what can happen when the truth gets out. Some people may think I'm crazy but I have a vision for things. I see it.

Imagine this church, with me as the pastor. Jay-Z as an evangelist and DMX as assistant pastor who would do a jail ministry. Can you see Lil' Kim and Nas doing the singles ministry and Puff leading the choir? Oh my goodness! You just think about that. Just let that sit in your mind for a minute. That's not even farfetched with the God that I serve.

I don't know how it's going to happen. But I believe it. I can see it even if it's not at my church.

I can see Nas as a deacon. The deacons are normally the cool dudes who shake hands and collect donations. "Yo, how you doing, son?" he would say to members of the congregation as they walked into church.

I can see it. I can see DMX in the jail ministry, doing great work with the wild people, the ones who think they can't be changed. When they come out they will need someone who understands their story. No matter how powerful they are, they can get saved.

And Lil' Kim. Yes! That would be a huge blessing, especially to the young women who have destructive backgrounds to know they can change. I can see her totally making an impact in the church. That's all we need is one more to come on out. With me doing what I'm doing, it's easy for people to dismiss it and say, "Mason's crazy." In the

Bible, the righteous always stood alone and the majority went the wrong way.

Some of these artists, you could see them being saved. Oh my goodness! What would 112 be like as a gospel group? What would Faith Evans be as a gospel singer? Not one song but a whole gospel album, leaving secular alone for good? Be with the Lord, 100 percent. What about Kelly Price, Brandy, Mariah Carey? Even Whitney Houston or Brian McKnight? How would they be as gospel singers? Can you imagine?

What would Biggie or Tupac have been like as pastors?

But when they come, they've got to surrender all. That's the problem; people try to keep something from their old self. The only reason I've been able to stay is because I was willing to give it all up and let Jesus take it from there. You would think by now, several years later, I would be back if I was insincere. But no, God is using me and I have to always give him the credit. I have to acknowledge that He's the One. He's taken me in front of intelligent people, those who have a plethora of things, and he's using me as a vessel.

People want to know how I'm doing all of this. How are all these healings and miracles taking place and I haven't even been here that long? How is that happening? All kinds of habits removed and they're trying to figure out how God is doing this through me when they know how I used to be. That's just God.

One Sunday one of Bad Boy's artists visited my church. "You really preach." She was surprised. The last time she saw me, I was high out of my mind. I know there was somebody else exposed to the truth that wasn't ready to make that move. You can feel they're not happy where they are. And I can tell them from experience that the best way to leave it is to just do it. Let God do the rest.

It's possible to come out of darkness and head into the light and end up in the shade, trying to compromise. There's no compromise with God. There ain't no middle place. It's either heaven or hell. It's either you're living or you're dead. You can't be half pregnant. Or halfway high. You're either pregnant or you're not. You're either high or you're sober. When you come to the Lord it's all or nothing.

Through me God doesn't draw the church people. He draws the church people who are sick of church—sick of going to church because it's just the same old thing to them. Neither does God draw the people who want to know him. When people come to see me preach it's usually the ones who'll say, "Ma$e is preaching?! Yo, I got to go see this!" Or it's the youth who want to see Ma$e.

But when they get there, the hardest dude and the most argumentative one will be at the altar sniffling, trying to keep it cool, not understanding what's overtaking them. They are the ones giving their lives over to God in the church God has placed me over. The Bible says that you know a tree by the fruit it bears. I'm here to be fruitful—to lead souls to Christ. I'm here to tell the truth.

For a good tree bringeth not forth corrupt fruit; neither doth a corrupt tree bring forth good fruit.

For every tree is known by his own fruit. For of thorns men do not gather figs, nor of a bramble bush gather they grapes.

A good man out of the good treasure of his heart bringeth forth that which is good: and an evil man out of the evil treasure of his heart bringeth forth that which is evil: for of the abundance of the heart his mouth speaketh.

—LUKE 6:43-45

Sermon

*N*ow I'm going to tell you something about a tree. A tree that
stands there that's not a fig tree has leaves. Not only does it
have leaves, but it will have a bird's nest. Not only does it have a
bird's nest, but it will have birds. Not only will it have birds, but
the birds are making more birds. The tree is flourishing. It's telling
you that "he that keepeth the fig tree shall eat the fruit thereof." So
now when the tree starts to flourish not only does it have leaves, but
it has fruit. But it started off as a fig tree. It started off with
nothing on it. Now as a fig tree, I have to shake the crows off.

Who are the crows?

The people who see me with nothing, who are always telling me
I'm not going to be nothing because my father wasn't nothing and
all of those things. Because right now, I'm a fig tree. All I have
right now is what God promised me.

I don't have the things I used to have, but I'm standing on
God's promise. I'm standing as a fig tree.

Now he's standing as a fig tree, which means he's standing with
nothing. A fig tree doesn't have what it wants, or it wouldn't be a
fig tree. Once a fig tree starts flourishing, you got the birds, your
birds having birds, you got the nest. You got the squirrel coming
through, trying to get a nut. You got all the way up, monkeys
swinging on the tree. And an owl. Because the tree became
prosperous, now it's got an owl on the tree.

(sermon continued on page 129)

PART TWO

New Testament

The Light

What! know ye not that he which is joined to a harlot is one body? for two, saith he, shall be one flesh.

But he that is joined unto the Lord is one spirit.

— 1 Corinthians 6:16-17

EIGHT

Lost and Found

I was partying at the Mirage in New York City, dancing with this chick. She was dancing real freaky.

"What you gonna do?" I said jokingly.

And then she grabbed my hand. She was too thirsty. I never thought she would get down like that.

The next thing I know, we're in the hotel. I was a young dude at the time, wilder than you could ever imagine. And I gave her something to talk about.

That's how I was treating women back then, when I was Ma$e. After a while there were girls making me the talk of the town. That worked in my favor. It wasn't like I was just messing with the bourgie chicks—most entertainers only messed with the light-skinned skinny women, or that model type. That wasn't me. I'd take a hood chick over a model chick any day.

I always felt if you got a hood chick, you got her. Once you got her sprung, she was going to do whatever. Once you got into any woman's mind, you got her. She knows what it's like to struggle. And when you struggling, she's more likely to hang with you.

I understood a little of psychology from a couple of classes I took in college. And I was well versed in street psychology. You put the book knowledge together with the street knowledge and you have a powerful combination. I had both. And that meant women didn't have a chance.

I would tell them a portion of the truth and a portion of what they wanted to hear. Part of the truth is that they wanted to be with me, and that they wanted me to be with them, and only them. I gave them part of the truth—I may cheat, but not with everyone. They were special.

"No matter how many mistakes I make, when it's over, it's gonna be me and you," I would say. And they would hold out hoping that was true.

Just as women get caught out there, following behind men promising half-truths, people get caught out there following doctrines that are half-truths. The problem is people don't make it their business to know the truth for themselves. So when someone comes along telling them something that sounds about right, they follow it. If you don't read the Bible and a person tells you something from the Bible, but they say it out of context or twist it around, then you might go with it because you don't know.

How many people get led astray on false doctrine and by stuff that sounds "about right"? They want to believe it. They want salvation, but they don't want to find out the truth for themselves. They follow that partial truth because it's what they *want* to hear. It's the same thing with a woman. She gets caught up because she is willing to believe what she wants to hear is true. She doesn't really want to know the whole truth.

The truth is, I never respected women until I got saved. It got to the point where I was just developing a reputation with the ladies—it was about my ego at that point. Women were there to feed my ego.

I didn't even need game. I had game, but once I became M-A-$-E, I never needed to show it. It's like any basketball superstar. He can walk on the court and people know what he can do. He doesn't have to prove anything. Once you get to a certain status you don't need game, you just need to be bold. All I had to do was walk into the room and speak what I wanted into existence. I would be in a club dancing and just shout out, "Who wants to go home with me?" and a few girls would come over and accept the invitation.

I would say, "Get your friends, get your coat and come on!" When I got so large, I would tell them to leave their coat just to show I had mind control.

That's why you never see stars at a party long.

We'd hit a city. We'd be in a mall, see some girls, and say, "What's up?" Girls would want to know, "Where's the party at?" And we'd give them the hotel and room number. In every city there would be new girls.

We would go out and do shows and have our own security guards check IDs at the hotel elevators. Only those who were of age were let up. On our floor—which was usually the whole floor—girls would be running around naked and you could just pick who you wanted.

These women would give us their numbers and want us to call the next time we'd be in town. How easy was that? Some would fly to New York just to hang out. Some girls were just freaky—they would do absolutely anything. Seeing this made me have the lowest respect for women.

When I was just regular old Mason, if I looked at a girl wrong, she would smack me. But as Ma$e, she may say, "Stop playing," and then minutes later she would be down for whatever, and I mean *whatever*. Did I transform into another man? Did I get more handsome or more charming? My game didn't change. It was ridiculous the lengths some of these women would go to just to sleep with me.

And it got to a point where the stakes had to get higher for me to even have fun. It had to get wilder and wilder.

Atlanta: That was the spot. My man introduced me to this house where all the hottest strippers in Atlanta would be. It was like a brothel but for my generation. I would take my boy there and I even took the whole group from Harlem World and I was the talk for months.

And that got boring.

I was introduced by a record executive to this spa. And it looked just like what I imagined a spa was. I figured I needed to relax a little and I had never been to a spa before, so I was with it. I went into this room and they had me take off my clothes and they give me a nice towel to put around myself.

I got up on the table thinking, "I'm about to get a massage. This is going to be the joint—two women giving me a massage."

This beautiful girl comes in. She looks half-Asian, half-black and starts giving me a massage and it's feeling real good. And when she's done, she paused and said, "What else

119

do you want?" At first, I'm thinking, "I must be a real charming dude." Then she says, "Roll over. Do you want me to finish?"

I started looking around the room like, "You can't be serious!" She made a gesture like what else do you want. And I said, "Oh! What else do I want?" And I found out everything she was willing to do.

After that, whenever I was in Atlanta I made sure I gave myself some time for the "spa." It was perfect for me. I could get exactly what I wanted without any hassles. I had gotten to the point where I didn't want to be bothered with the whole drama of dealing with them—putting them in a cab, feeding them, talking to them. It was too much maintenance.

It was an Oriental place with beautiful women. Most of the girls there looked mixed and they wore Oriental gowns. There was a small waterfall inside and nice, calming music. You could do anything to them. After the girls found out who I was it seemed like it was pleasure for them to please me.

And it seemed like it took more and more for me to find pleasure. I had done just about everything you can imagine— black chicks, white chicks, two's and three's. After all of that where do you go from there?

With all the bad I was doing, I kept wanting to do more. Distraction leads you farther down the road of destruction. I began spending a lot of time in spas and strip joints. I had some real wild times in the strip joints.

But that's how I was living. I was out of my mind. I was insane. I met this young lady at the Golden Lady—she was stripping. She was trying to mess with me while I was in there, walking around with a few dollars in her G-string and I said, "What you doin' in here? You look like a baby." She told me she was working, getting paid but what she really wanted to do was rap.

"Get dressed and let's go," I told her. I took her out of that club. She couldn't wait to leave. I don't think she ever went back after that. Now she's one of the hottest female rappers in the game today.

I don't have a relationship with her, but I know how powerful God is. I know He has a plan for her.

You know what's so scary? The women I used to be with in all those cities actually considered what I was doing to them was love. Even after I got saved, these women would still call.

"I just want to come see you," they would say. I was like, "Nah. I ain't as strong as I need to be. You might have me going in the wrong direction." And they would for sure. It was a life I had to quit cold turkey. I found out that I couldn't wean myself from girls a little bit at a time.

The girls were the hardest thing to give up. Even though I changed the lifestyle, going to church and hanging with church folks, the girls were still present. I could give up weed because there was no weed in the church and nobody's smoking in front of me. I could give up drinking because there's no drinking in the church. But women? They are plentiful in the church. I was getting more looks from church girls than from sinners sometimes.

Now I'm celibate. I have to be celibate. A little bit of sex will have me in a whole lot of sin.

When I first started going to church and studying, I wasn't

celibate. I was still struggling with women. I couldn't understand why I couldn't stop. The women would still be there ready and willing—even in church. I was going to one church and when people found out I was going, they started going, too. Here I am trying to change and the devil was still presenting me with temptations. I wasn't strong enough to say no at first.

Every time I would fall, I kept saying to God, "This is my last time."

People don't understand why I'm so hard on that stuff—why I cannot tolerate sexual immorality. Because I know what it can do to you. I used to be sitting there saying, "This is my last time" and thought I meant it. But the next one becomes my last time. And I meant that, too. Then I was just masturbating and getting oral sex, thinking I was okay with God. I used to think that oral sex wasn't sex—that it wasn't a sin. I thought I could get away with it. But I was wrong.

The thing that made it finally my last time was when God showed me that He wanted to use me in a mighty way, and if I didn't stop, he couldn't use me at all. He also showed me that just because you go to church doesn't mean you're going to heaven. I'll say it again: *Just because you're going to church doesn't mean you're going to heaven.* People need to understand this. I would help people get saved, but their life wouldn't change. I would lead people to Christ, but they wouldn't change. I was operating in a dirty lifestyle and they couldn't be totally set free. Which would mean they would be back at the altar praying about the same things.

When I first started I was struggling. I couldn't understand why that lust demon wouldn't be shook. Why was that feeling still there? God was showing me that I was putting myself around lustful people. The time came for me to say, "I want all that God's got for me." I just started being celibate.

But I needed help. I walked into the church office and I told the pastor, "I need help." I told God, "I need help." I didn't tell them what I needed help about, I just told them I needed help. I was keeping it real, all the way real. I believe I was having sex so much, feeding that spirit of lust so long, that I couldn't stop. You feed something long enough and it becomes strong and powerful and hard to control.

I would do it and then get mad at the woman and say, "You know I'm trying to live right. You know better." But I was the one who really knew better.

I fasted and prayed. And I still couldn't stop.

Why can't I stop?!

When I finally got to the point where I wanted to throw up after any sexual contact, I knew I had enough strength to change. I drove to Siloam Baptist. I pulled into the parking lot, got out of the car, and fell to my knees right there. I was so disgusted.

God told me to pick up two rocks off the ground and remember that this is the ground you have been delivered on. He said, "The next time you ever do it . . . you're fired."

I wrote a message and put it up. When God gave me a church, I preached it in my church. I carry those rocks in my pocket. God wanted me to remember the agreement we made. In the Bible anything that was built on the rock couldn't fall. So those rocks have a lot of meaning to me.

Everything you build on the rock will succeed. Ever since then, the ministry took off. God started showing me favor. I started getting back everything I lost from music. Now I'm getting everything from God.

Before this I would preach and people would be getting saved. But God showed me in the Scripture where many people who cast out demons and healed people in Jesus' name in the end, He said, "Depart from me, I never knew you."

I wanted God to know me. I want my name to be in that Book of Life.

I started making integrity my policy. I'm going to tell the truth, the whole truth, no matter who it offends.

Then God gave me a fiancée. I plan on marrying before the end of the year. God wouldn't show me her until I first kicked the habit and started living with integrity. Integrity is not lying to yourself. Integrity is knowing who you are in the dark—the person people can't see. Integrity is being real in those dark places where it's just you and God and bringing everything into the light.

Integrity is knowing something is wrong and fixing it before you get caught. Because if you change only after you get caught doing something wrong, that's worldly sorrow. Integrity is being able to check yourself.

You won't see all God has for you until you have integrity. He didn't want me to get married until I kicked the habit because if I didn't, I would have married the wrong person or gotten married for the wrong reasons.

For the longest time I couldn't accept that there was only one woman for me. When I first got saved, I said, "Solomon had a bunch of concubines and he was a man of God. Let me chill like that."

But God had other plans. He had a different life for me. And I accepted this.

And the rib, which the LORD *God had taken from man, made he a woman, and brought her unto the man.*

And Adam said, This is *now bone of my bones, and flesh of my flesh: she shall be called Woman, because she was taken out of man.*

—GENESIS 2:22-23

Sermon

*N*ow *who is the owl? The owl is supposed to be the one who's the most wise. But it's always saying what? "Who?!" Who got this on? Who got that on? Who giving the sermon? Who going to sing today? Who church is this? Who?*

The owl is supposed to be the wisest thing on the tree but all he is saying is, "Who?"

Somebody come in and don't look right. Who is that? Who? Who? Now the tree is flourishing. Before the tree was flourishing you never saw the owl in the tree. You never saw monkeys trying to come down the tree and mess up the tree. They're just swinging, doing their thing. They don't care what fruit they knock off the tree. You got monkeys in the tree of God. They're just swinging through the church. They don't care who they offend, whose feelings they hurt because now the tree is flourishing. When it was by itself, (the tree) didn't have nothing; it never had none of those problems. Never. But when you get big, that's when everybody's got something to say.

Then there's the squirrel. Now I'm still on "Hell is never full." But I have to build you up to that point.

The squirrel just wants a fig. The squirrel ain't really about the tree, it's just there to take what it can. It's there to get a fig. You have people who come to church to meet people. Come to church to meet girls. Come to church to meet guys. Those are the squirrels in the church.

(sermon continued on page 143)

NINE

Flesh of My Flesh

I met my fiancée during a prayer service in church. We were walking in a circle praying. And when I opened my eyes she was just standing right there. God was telling me to open my eyes, he had something special for me to see.

I was praying to God. And God showed me, "What I have for you is right in front of you." I opened my eyes and she was walking and praying. When she sat down, I went over to talk to her after the service. And everything I was thinking was coming out of her mouth. There was a gentle boldness that I admired.

She said, "When I was walking past you the spirit was so strong and I couldn't understand what it was."

Something was telling me to hug her. But I was thinking, "I can't hug this girl, I don't even know her." Then I thought, "She ain't for me."

She started talking to me about her job. She was a consultant for some big company in Atlanta making fifty dollars an hour. She graduated from UCLA with a degree in chemical engineering. I figured she had to be smart to have a masters in that.

She said she wasn't happy and she was thinking about taking the day off to find out what God was saying to her. She said He was trying to show her something.

"If God is showing you something, you need to see what it is," I said.

She took the day off, and that evening she came to our Wednesday service.

"Why don't you just quit that job and come work in the ministry," I said. "All we got to give you is three hundred a week."

"You know what?" she said. "I was thinking about doing that anyway."

Her job kept asking her to travel on Wednesdays and do presentations for the company. That kept her away from church on Wednesday. She told her bosses that she couldn't travel much anymore because she was about to have a family.

"Are you married? Are you engaged? Or pregnant?" I asked her. But I'm knowing what's up the whole time.

"No," she said. "But God told me I was going to have a family soon."

And what she was saying was scaring me because I heard the same thing from God. It scared me so bad that I stopped being around her. I started thinking, "This woman is into voodoo or *Roots* or something."

But God told me to keep speaking to her. So I did. At this time, she was still thinking about leaving her job. She said, "I feel like I'm wasting my life there."

"If it's not God's will, you're really wasting your time," I told her.

Then she said, "God is telling me that somebody is supposed to share something with me and they're not being obedient."

She was *really* scaring me. And I stopped hanging around her again for good—so I thought. But I couldn't stay away.

We decided to get her work in the offices of S.A.N.E. Ministries, building our Website. We already had someone who was supposed to be doing it, but it was her specialty. I went home that night and I prayed about it. And when I got to the office the next day, the person originally assigned to do our Website told me, "I don't think this job is for me."

So she got the job. But there was still one problem. I was the one not telling her what God was telling me—that she was the one. When that came through my spirit I was like, "Oh, no! I'm still young. I want to wait."

As a man you think as soon as you settle down, all of the good ones are going to be coming out of the woodwork. I knew she was everything, but I still was afraid—knowing the past—that I would never be satisfied.

God told me, "Men are not going to be responsible until you become responsible. You teach everybody else to trust in the Lord. You say you trust Me but now you're trying to understand Me. You say you believe Me but now you're trying to understand what I'm doing. That woman is the one for you."

And God was right. I mean, she is everything I've ever wanted in a woman.

"You say you want a woman who loves the Lord. Well, she really loves Me," God said. "You say you want a woman who is smart, well, she's very smart," God said. "You want a woman who's real nice but can be bold . . . that's her. You want someone who is good looking? She's beautiful. I'm giving you

132

everything you want in one package without one thing missing and you're still sitting up here praying.

"If you pick the wrong woman, you will be living in the wrong state, in the wrong house, with the wrong kids going to the wrong school. Getting the wrong education and you end up with the wrong job, with the wrong salary driving the wrong car. You will end up with the wrong life—all because you're not listening to the one thing I'm telling you now."

My fiancée, Twyla, was everything I ever wanted. In my life I have had maybe four serious girlfriends—Kiki, Brandy, Sameko, and Diane—all four of them were all very different but I liked each one a lot. Twyla has all of the best qualities of every woman I ever liked.

She is real cool and down to earth like Sameko. She is smart like Diane. She will do anything for me like Kiki. And the people love her like Brandy. The enemy was trying to give me pieces. In actuality all I had to do was wait on God and I got all of what I wanted in one package.

I have to keep it real; if I were still in the world, my fiancée would still hold up under scrutiny. Twyla's beautiful in every sense of the word—the type you don't mind holding your hand in the mall. But none of those qualities—even together in a package—would have been enough for her to be my wife.

The fact that she loves God is what qualifies her to be my wife.

And she loves God more than life. I knew she was the one and, knowing that, I had to do something about it. So I called her up and we met at the church.

"I can't promise that we're going to be rich," I said. "And I don't know what the future holds for us. I just know I need you in it."

She got real emotional. I know people get on one knee and all that, but that's not me. I ain't really good with the romantic stuff. I just had to tell her what I was thinking, straight up.

"All I have is God's promises," I said. "Is that enough for you?"

She said "yes" about ten times.

I said. "You know I'm a difficult person to deal with?" She said she didn't care.

"You know I don't have money for a ring?" I said. She said she didn't care.

We went to pick out her ring. The man at the jewelry store showed us three different rings. And I asked her which one did she want. "That's not my job to pick out the ring," she said. She passed step one.

"Do you like this one?" I asked, pointing to the biggest thing in the showcase. I then put down that ring and picked up the smallest ring and I looked at her to see if her face changed. I wanted to see if she would be disappointed that I put down the five-carat ring for the half-carat. But her expression didn't change one bit. She passed step two.

So I picked the smallest ring and said, "What I have for you is way beyond this ring." I put the ring on her finger. She jumped on me like we hit Lotto or something. And when the guy came back with the bill, she paid for it. And passed step three.

When we left the store, I stopped at a bank and gave her money back, all of it. And a couple of months later I put the big carat ring on her finger to replace the tiny one. The Bible says if you're faithful with a little, you'll be faithful with much.

I'm happy with my fiancée. Marriage ain't something to play with. You've got to know. For a couple of weeks after we got engaged, we were going to church and no one knew. And God kept saying to me, "Be responsible." How could I expect to lead a church and bring men into the kingdom if I couldn't be obedient or was afraid of losing my congregation?

"You have her walking around being engaged but everyone thinks you're single," God said.

It was cool being single. The freedom. But God said, "You've got to do it." Not that I was forced into it.

On May 20, 2001, I announced to my church that Twyla McInnis would soon be Mrs. Betha. Once I said it, I could feel the mood change in the congregation. And afterward it was confirmed. Normally after church, people would be outside fellowshipping. But on this Sunday, everybody bounced. Normally more people would stay to talk to me, or at least say, "Hi." But I guess this was the day I was supposed to go straight home.

God said, "Only those who are here for the Word will stay."

Before this, a lot of people were coming to church for the wrong reasons. I knew all along what I was supposed to do. But I had just started the ministry and I thought all of my members were going to leave if I got married. I have a church full of women and I was thinking that most of them were only there because I was a single man. There would be no more extra "Hallelujahs" and "Amens" when I preached on Sunday.

The following Sunday our congregation went from two hundred members to about eighty. And I can say that I'm glad.

I think it was beneficial to the church. It's like pruning a garden. You have to get rid of the dead stuff in your garden so new things can grow.

The message I preached that Sunday was, "Take ownership." I talked about responsibility—about men stepping up and being more responsible, being more responsible in their lives, and becoming men who will take care of their family and not rely on someone else to do it.

I said that men needed to stop holding people responsible for the way their lives turned out. I hear people talk about, "The devil made me do it." The devil didn't do it. You did it. He may have made things available, tempted you with an opportunity, but he can't make you *do* anything.

Then there are those who blame their father. "My father wasn't there for me," they say. Okay, but is that any excuse for why you need to follow in his footsteps and not be there for your kids or the woman in your life? And I'm not saying that as a man you can't make any mistakes. We all make mistakes. We're human. But a man takes responsibility for his mistakes. Real men own up to them, they try to fix them. Don't just sit in your error, do something about it. Ask for help.

David is a great example of a man who made mistakes and still was able to find favor with God because he owned up to it. He asked for help.

He said, "It's me, oh Lord!" David was able to change because he took responsibility for what he did. He didn't say, "It was someone else, oh Lord," or "The devil made me do it, oh Lord," or "It was the woman's fault, oh Lord." He could have made excuses for why he slept with Bathsheba. She was married to another man and it could have been easy to say that she knew she had a husband so it was her fault. But he didn't. He said, "It's me oh Lord, standing in the need of help."

Excuses will never get you into the kingdom of heaven.

Real men stand up and take responsibility—not only for their own actions but for the things around them.

I learned this from a strong man, Samuel Dixon. My mother married Samuel Dixon and he was the only father I ever knew.

I had so much respect for him because he walked into a situation with five kids who were not his and he took on the responsibility of a father—as the head of the house. He made sure that we had everything we needed.

He used to work at Nine West in their corporate offices, and my sisters and moms were always getting hooked up with free shoes. He would take us all to the company picnics. We were his family. He came to our family with a son, and my mother never made a distinction. He was our brother just as the five of us were Samuel's kids.

Samuel and my mother had their problems—what couple doesn't?—but it was nothing hot water couldn't get rid of.

He treated us like his in every way. He put a roof over our heads, clothes on our backs, and if we needed it, discipline. And this from somebody whose loins I didn't come from, would even beat us if we got out of hand. I never really had to get any beatings because he and I had an understanding. First, I had the opportunity to watch my other brothers and sisters get in trouble.

This was a guy who just said, "I see an opportunity to be with this woman and I'm not." He understood as a man that he could strengthen her in the areas that she was weak, and vice versa. That's about knowing you're the man for the job, stepping up to the plate and getting that job done.

Samuel, whose nickname is Lucky, taught me most of the things I know today. His most important lesson was to go with my gut instinct—go with what I know deep in my heart. "If you do that you won't have any regrets about anything you do," he said.

He used to take me out and we'd watch basketball together. He even taught me how to play basketball when I was little. There was a time when I couldn't beat him. But now I can crush him (don't tell him I said that). We had a bunch of great times together. Me and him saw eye-to-eye. We knew who we were to each other—it was everybody else who didn't catch on to the fact that he was really our father.

When my brothers and sisters would get in trouble and Samuel had to chastise them, they would have to let out a "You ain't my father!" every now and then. I wouldn't blame Samuel if he had said, "Well, go find your father then." They would have these dreams that one day our biological father would return, and they would say, "I can't wait until my father comes back." And Samuel would say jokingly, "We all can't wait until your father comes back."

He was our father. I give no credit to my biological father. He was just a donor.

I was blessed with two examples of a man—how to be, and how not to be.

Samuel made our family gel—he made it complete. He was the missing piece to our family. No matter how strong a woman is, there's nothing like a male presence to lend stability to a household.

It's like a church without God there. No matter how many people are there, no matter how much money they collect, no matter how big that church is—without the Father, it's not the house of God.

A bunch of kids in the house without a father is a dysfunctional family. I call on men to be responsible so kids don't have to have a single-parent family. Many kids who grow up in a home without a father sometimes grow up without knowing how to be a father themselves.

It's hard. I know it's hard. But men need to step up and be men. Take care of your children. And if you're with a woman who has children, make those children your own. I am grateful that I have a father. He paved the way for me to become the man I am today. He helped me to know how a man is supposed to raise a family.

Every day I wake up, I'm amazed. "I'm really an effective pastor," I say to myself. And if I think about becoming discouraged, God lets me know He's with me. I'm just blessed to know that God loves me. That's the best feeling in the world to know that God is happy about what you do. And I thank God for that.

And I thank God that I don't have to take this journey alone. I have Twyla.

Now don't get me wrong, there is plenty of temptation out there. And women still try me. Young ladies will come up to me and say, "My friend wants to talk to you." I'm proud to say, "You're somebody else's blessing."

And it feels so good. It makes me feel grown up to say, "Sweetheart, I'm taken." And mean it.

Now I say, "I got a wife," and they back off like, "Oh,

okay." It shocks them. Because Ma$e was never taken. Ma$e was never a one-woman man. Ma$e was never really a man. He was trying to take other dudes' girls. He was trying to corrupt a girl who went to church and tried to do right. Just to see. Just to test his manhood. But that ain't being a man at all. That's being a coward.

Marriage was a word that would have scared Ma$e to death. Mason is looking forward to it. Mason is taken.

And the LORD *God formed man of the dust of the ground, and breathed into his nostrils the breath of life; and man became a living soul.*

—GENESIS 2:7

Sermon

*I*t says, *"whoso keepeth the fig tree shall eat the fruit thereof. So he who waiteth on his master, shall be honored."* Not might be. Not maybe. But shall *be honored. He that waiteth on his master shall be honored. What does waiteth mean?*

My brother, I tell him, "I will wait for you until three o'clock." Which means if he's not there by three o'clock and if he's not there, I'm going. Waiting for my brother until three o'clock means that I'm going to give him a grace period until three-fifteen and if he's not there then, I'm going to leave. Waiting on my brother until three o'clock means, I waited and he didn't come and it didn't seem like he was coming, so I left. So those are the natural "waits." What is waiteth? Waiteth is consistency. Waiteth is faithfulness. Waiteth is not wait. It's the three letters at the end—the e-t-h. Waiteth. To God, "waiteth" is patience. It means if God told me He's going to do it, He's going to do it. If the landlord tells me I have three months to get this money or else I'm going to get kicked out, I have to waiteth on God. Waiteth. Patience, faithfulness, consistency is waiteth. That doesn't mean that tomorrow is the time the money is due and I don't have it and it don't look like God's going to do it, so I might as well get this money myself. That's not waiteth.

'Cause God is not going to raise men and women who are not going to waiteth. You have so many people telling other people, "He that waiteth on the Lord, his strength shall be renewed." But you're not waiteth.

How are you going to tell me, "God will make a way," and "God's going to do this," but then when bad things come in your life, you crying. Ain't you the same one who told me, "God will make a way?"

Are you waiteth or have you been waiting?

(sermon continued on page 161)

TEN

God-made Man

I'm in a room full of preachers—old and young—and they're asking me why should I be ordained.

"What are you going to add to the Kingdom?" a pastor asked.

"Are you sure this is something God is telling you to do?" asked another. "What's your purpose?"

"God has called me for the generation that everyone is having a hard time reaching—who seem to be uncontrollable, the ones who don't believe anything unless they see it," I responded.

I got quizzed on The Word and they kept giving questions until they were satisfied with my answers. It made me feel as though my ordination was determined by man, but I knew in my heart that these men were inspired by God. You can go to school and have degrees in religion and not be ready to be ordained.

And after much examination, they deemed me credible. Then a pastor preached a sermon to bring me into the ministry. I was preached into a new life, a new level of God.

On May 20, 2001—exactly one year after I gave my first sermon, I received my honorary doctorate of theology from St. Paul's. I am officially Pastor Mason Betha.

Bishop Wayne T. Jackson, of Great Faith Ministries in Detroit, made one statement to me that I don't think he knew how powerful it was.

He said, "Look at me, I used to be a dope addict. I used to be a pimp. I went to jail and look at me now. I'm a God-made man."

That clicked in my mind as well as in my heart. If I didn't hear another thing while we were speaking for three hours, that one statement stood out. "I'm a God-made man." You never want to be a person where the people make you. When they do, it's shortly thereafter that they try to get you up out of there. They build you up to take you out. We live in a contemporary society. Con-Temporary. It's "con," meaning deceitful for personal gain. And it's temporary, meaning a fad, a phase, a moment, a myth; it will fade away.

Everything is temporary and oftentimes you've been conned into believing that man's values are the definition of success. And what you've come to believe is good isn't necessarily good *for* you.

I think it's important to remember where you came from because God can use people and their experiences to help people come to Him. Men like Bishop Jackson and men like me. God sent out all types of men from all types of backgrounds to spread His Word. But they all had something in common—they surrendered all to be with Him. When Jesus called His disciples, the fishermen had to drop their nets, they had to stop whatever they were doing and follow Him immediately. They had to leave their families and follow Him.

When God called, you had to go. There were some others, like Abraham, who had to leave the town that was familiar to them in order to please God. And Jesus said that a prophet is never accepted in his own land—he will be loved everywhere but home.

No matter how high God takes you, there will be some people who want to hold on to the old you. For them, letting go of the old you means that God can change you. And if God can change you, then God can change them, and many people are afraid of being changed. Holding on to the old you is their way of not changing.

When you come to Christ, you have to surrender something. Those who are used greatly, they had to come away from the very things that made them. In our times, everyone is trying to come away from what they're doing without leaving anything. And if you're going to take the things the devil gave you with you, you can't serve God—at least not sincerely. Your body can't be in the church while your mind is on something at home.

I love Christ with my actions. Christ has been so good to me, the least I can do is love Him with my actions. I've been going around this whole entire world, just preaching. I used to get discouraged that people didn't reach out to help. But I'm glad they didn't because at that time God was teaching me to depend solely on Him.

He also was showing me that He wanted me to do the uncommon thing. And He wanted me to stay uncommon. "I want you to stay rare," He said. No one wants what's com-

147

mon. Everyone's looking for the rarest thing, the thing that stands out. Why should it be different with Christ?

It's not for me to become a clone of any preacher out there. If I'm going to do something different, I've got to go about it in a different way. I don't desire to have a television ministry. Right now, it's not for me. They may be wonderful and I'm sure many people get saved. But that's not what God wanted me to do first.

I wouldn't feel comfortable having this church with lots of stained glass, bright lights, a twelve-piece orchestra and fancy purple-and-gold-trimmed robes with a congregation dressed in their finest clothes and expensive pearls. I couldn't see me having a place that a crackhead or dope dealer wouldn't come in. My church has to make a prostitute feel welcome. God wants to reach those people, too, and they can't be reached in the usual way.

I'm going to do it the way God instructed me to—in an *unusual* way.

How do I know God is speaking to me? I know because His voice is distinctive. It's not always loud, neither is it the deep voice that Moses heard at the burning bush while receiving the Ten Commandments as seen on television. Sometimes God's voice can speak through pain and disappointment. When He speaks, it's so clear that even a baby can understand. And His message never involves confusion.

I remember God's voice becoming stronger and clearer when I moved into my new house in Atlanta. I had to leave the old house—the one Ma$e bought—because it had too many memories of that old life. And God provided a new house.

I was in my new house, in my new bathroom, sitting in my

my gym shorts and a black tank top on the edge of the Jacuzzi meditating, getting ready for my day. I was asking God, "What am I doing? What is all of this about?"

I had given up my life to the Lord. I separated myself from the people. I've gone to church for what seemed like the longest time.

"Lord, where am I going? What am I doing?" I asked.

And I heard the words, "Why does it matter? You're with Me. I am in control."

When you're not with God, you're wandering aimlessly anyway. But people don't ever think about that. Or maybe they don't care. But if you think before you set out on a trip, you usually bring directions with you to make sure you don't get lost. Why shouldn't you use directions for your life to make sure you don't get lost on your way to heaven?

God makes his directions so plain and simple—all we have to do is follow. But too many of us want to know "Why" or want to try to understand the path God has chosen for us. Maybe this is why I became frustrated. I was spending too much time trying to understand God instead of flowing with what God was doing.

But after He spoke to me, I surrendered.

I started doing whatever He said, no matter how crazy it seemed. Some days God would send me to church with a message that says, "Everybody needs to repent!" And that would be the message. Not a word more. And all sorts of people from various lifestyles would come up and get saved with no sermon, no long message, no songs.

One time I was visiting a church in New Mexico, and I was telling the people that the Lord wants us to sincerely surrender. I told them that God wants us to lie facedown and cry out to Him. God said, "If My people, which are called by My Name, would just humble themselves and turn from their wicked ways." I was trying to show the congregation there is no way to turn from their wicked ways without first humbling themselves.

"We don't want to be arrogant Christians," I said. "You can't be carrying yourselves in an arrogant way, where you are perceiving yourself almost like a celebrity."

And the people just laid out on the floor. I mean, everybody laid out. And when they got up they were feeling totally free. Many of the strongholds were broken that day. And I am so grateful. God didn't have to use me. He knows people are watching. So He brings me in front of those curious people and does miraculous things.

My life is an avenue for God to do something great. God also knows that He will get the glory from the work He is doing through me. I wish there were more men in the music industry, pornography industry, drug-dealing industry, who would let God make them, who would just give Christ one try. Just try God.

I say give God the same try you gave smoking. I tell young women, "Give Christ the same shot you gave that man. You didn't try to understand him. Anything he told you to try once, you tried it. You didn't ask questions, you gave it a try."

When you love somebody—even in a worldly love—you do things for them that you wouldn't normally do. So why can't you do the same for Christ. Trust God.

I trust the Lord. I had to trust Him. I was so far out from the boat—like Peter was—I *had* to trust. Peter trusted in the

Lord and was able to walk on water until he got scared and then he began to sink.

After finishing a sermon, Jesus sent his disciples ahead in a boat while he went to a mountain to pray. When He finished, the boat had gotten far into the sea. Jesus walked on the water out to the boat. Peter said, "Lord, if it's you, tell me to come to you in the water." And Jesus said, "Come." And Peter got out of the boat and walked on the water toward Jesus.

That was nothing but faith. Peter trusted in the Lord and he was able to perform the same miracle as Jesus. But then the seeds of doubt and fear got to him and Peter started to sink. He got scared. And had to cry out to the Lord for help.

Peter had faith. He just got scared. But he wasn't afraid to ask for help. You have to have the same faith—and when you are afraid or doubtful or discouraged, you have to be willing to call on the Lord for strength. He won't let you drown.

I had to trust in the Lord and not listen to the people and go back to the way I was living. How could I go back to the same things the Lord set me free from? I would be a fool to go back to being a puppet, especially for that puppet-master Satan. If I'm going to be used, I'm going to be used by God. Man is not going to use me for nothing. Man and Satan have gotten their work out of me—they can't get another moment.

That instantly made me God-made. I was no longer man-made.

I'm at a point right now where I'm like Paul. The Gentiles (the people in the secular world) don't want to let him go and the people in the church don't want to deal with him because they perceive him as being a threat. Paul used to kill Christians, so when he became one, the Christians were skeptical. I was a rapper and now I'm speaking against them and some people are skeptical.

The Bible said that once they realized Paul was really of God, he ended up being a bigger help to the church than the world. That's what I plan to be and all the glory will go to God. Because of where I come from, God can use me to lead people to the Kingdom that many think can't be saved, people who have been stubborn toward the Word.

A lady in my church, Sister Julia, gave me some good advice in this area. She told me that if I let the people make me a celebrity in the church, then I'm right back where I started, and that's not progress.

She said, "The devil will let you come to church if you're prideful. He will make you a superstar in the church if you're not careful."

She told me God wanted me to be cautious so I wouldn't be in a position for people to make me like last time.

I can walk into a church as Mason, and just because they think I'm Ma$e they give me more respect than anyone else in the church. That's a contradiction to God's word. God doesn't want me to be a star to the church. He wants me to be an angel. Both a star and an angel shine, but a star shines for the world, an angel shines for the Kingdom. I've shined enough for the secular world.

The hardest thing to give up besides women was to give up the old me. Getting rid of things is much easier than getting rid of an entire self. Eliminating Ma$e from my life took all the strength I had. It got to the point where if people started talking about Ma$e, I couldn't respond. He had to fade away and die.

I'm just writing about what I vaguely remember about him. Ma$e.

If I were still Ma$e, I definitely could not have been celibate. I couldn't do any of the things God has allowed me to do. With Ma$e, there's always a motive. You wouldn't want him in your church. When you think about how many children followed Ma$e, then you know how much influence he would have on that church—for the bad. For the devil.

Ma$e couldn't have a female friend—he would always have other motives. I didn't think it was possible to be "just friends" with a girl. But Roxanne Brown showed me that it was possible.

I met her just after I had gotten saved and I enrolled in Clark University to take some classes. I met Roxanne the first day and she was definitely the kind of girl that Ma$e would have been on in a heartbeat. She was serious and classy—a diva with short, blond, curly hair at the time I met her.

She was also in a sorority, the Deltas. But she wasn't just some ordinary Delta. It seemed like everybody in the Atlanta University Center—that included Clark, Morris Brown, Spelman, and Morehouse—knew Roxanne Brown.

When I approached her we instantly began to talk. But it wasn't about "Let me get your number" or "What're you doing after class?" We talked about real-life stuff, stuff that shapes destiny. We talked about her vision, like, "Where do you see your life going? What is your ultimate purpose of being here?" The kind of stuff that doesn't seem like good conversation these days.

We talked that day and continued our conversation later that night. And it was something different for both of us, which was refreshing. After a few conversations, we really started talking about the Lord, and Roxanne got caught up. She turned her life over to God. She denounced her Greek letters and folks thought she was going crazy.

"What happened to Roxanne?" they were asking. She did a complete 180-degree change. She went from short hair to long hair, loud to humble, and partying to praying. She caught a lot of persecution. People were talking about how she was only doing it to be with me.

And we did date while we were both members of Siloam Baptist Church. But we sat down and realized that we would make much better friends than a couple. She was the first female friend I ever had in the Kingdom. And now Roxanne is my sister in Christ.

Before I got engaged, people would say behind her back that Roxanne would leave the church if I ever got married. When I announced my engagement, Roxanne was one of my biggest supporters. She stuck by the church while the ones who said she would leave are now gone. To this day, Roxanne is one of the pillars that holds up S.A.N.E. Ministries. She is a blessing. That is all God's glory there.

There were others like her who illustrated how miraculous God is, how he can change people's lives instantly.

I met Jasper Littlejohn on Clark's track. I was running sprints to try to get into shape. After I finished I couldn't find my water bottle; the trainer had left with the Gatorade and it was like 100 degrees out there. Then this dude comes over and starts asking me questions about Ma$e. He asked me why I left the music business—it was a question I heard a thousand times. And at first I was going to ignore him, but the look in his eyes told me he really needed to hear the answer and not for gossip.

He told me his name was Jasper Littlejohn and I thought that was hilarious. I told him why I left the business. "God is calling us to be men," I said. And I explained to him how the wrong music keeps us in a time that God wants us to be free from. There are spirits in music that control us—sometimes even for the bad. We have to break free from that. We stood there talking about God for a while.

Later on that night, Littlejohn was seen in the dorms, breaking every CD in his case. After that, he became like my little brother. I was schooling him about life and God—at least the little that I did know at the time—which broadened his perspective on everything. We would hang out every day, reading and studying the Bible. He would often hang out over at my house playing video games, so I told him to take one of the rooms in my house as his. Today he is a soldier for Jesus.

And so is DJ. He's from Delaware. I met him through my boy, Kev, who played basketball at the University of Georgia. Kev would be around when me and Jasper were talking about God and church. However, I never invited DJ to church. I don't know why I didn't; it just never crossed my mind to do so. One day I was talking to this young lady about Christ and DJ asked if he could go to church with me.

I thought he was frontin'. So many guys say, "Yeah, man. I'll go with you. But you got to call me, though. You got to wake me up. You know I be in the clubs all Saturday night." And when you get there to pick them up on Sunday, they holler out the window, "Ten more minutes!" You wait and blow the horn and they come back talking about, "Give me ten more minutes." And before you know it, service is over. The devil is so crafty.

But before Sunday came around, DJ ended up going to a Bible study on Wednesday. He was so moved that he brought his girlfriend, Allison, with him to church on Sunday. After the service he kept talking about how he was going to get his life right and how he was going to marry Allison. DJ did allow God to turn his life around. He was a dude who thought he was Allen Iverson—and DJ was a pretty good ball player. But he also looked like Iverson with the braids and the tattoo.

That quickly changed when he learned that man was made in the image of God—not Allen Iverson. He learned that you had to be the man that God made you. DJ cut off his braids, which were down his neck, and he began to totally change his look—*and* his life. Today he is married to Allison and is a pillar for S.A.N.E. Ministries.

But for every story of salvation, there is one of abandonment. The hardest thing sometimes about being saved is not having certain family members there to share in it. I lost so many people that I thought I always needed around—friends and other loved ones. But God taught me how to be a man. With His help, I learned how to stand alone.

Today, when I travel, I mostly go alone. Ma$e had an entourage with a publicist, an assistant, and a whole bunch of people. Mason travels alone—it's easier that way. It makes no sense building up a staff or an entourage if you know in the end it will on be you and God anyway. You come into this world alone and you leave it alone. And somewhere in the middle you had better learn how to *make* it on your own.

And if you continue to set good examples, maybe all of those people in your life who aren't saved will see that God truly does work. I don't want to give people any reason to turn their back on the Lord. It's sad to say, but there are many who are basing their decision to come to God on how things turn out for me. That's why I know God is going to do a great thing. He'll never allow them to say, "Remember Ma$e? He gave up all of that for God, now look at him! That God stuff don't pay off."

On the flip side, when they realize that my God provides, they'll be so on fire for God it won't be funny. As a result of my getting saved, God is working in my family. My brother Mike was first. Yeah, he had been in the streets, and he was very hotheaded. But he got saved. And once that happened, I was really convinced that anything could happen. He just came down to Atlanta and got saved. It was instant. Now he is in God's house, working for the Lord.

Stason was next. She was a tough one—hardheaded just like me. She had a lot of questions and didn't understand a lot of things at first.

She wanted to do music—even after I left it. I told her that the business wasn't about anything and that everybody was fake. She said, "Yeah, yeah. I still got to give it a try for my-self." But she saw that God wouldn't reward her stubbornness. Everything she tried to do in music failed.

Everybody goes through their stages of stubbornness where God's got to leave them there and let them see that nothing is going to change in their lives until they surrender.

Stason came to Atlanta with her daughter and she gave God a try. And she hasn't been the same since—she teaches in children's ministry church at Siloam Baptist, and it's been great for her.

People made Ma$e. God made Pastor Mason Betha. And when people make you, they can destroy you. What God has made, let no man put asunder.

Verily, verily, I say unto you, He believeth on me, the works that I do shall he do also; and greater works *than these shall he do; because I go unto my Father.*

—JOHN 14:12

Sermon

God told me I was going to be a great man of God when I was twelve years old. At that point, I stopped attending church regularly. So I didn't waiteth. I went and started focusing on music instead, because I was waiting and not waiteth. God is going to do everything He says He is going to do.

Now I'm going to deal with this word waiteth for a little longer because there are two sides to "waiteth." The Scriptures didn't say, He that waiteth on God. That's the interesting part. Since it does not read, He that waiteth on God, some people are waiting on the wrong things. It reads, He that waiteth on his master. If my master is not Jesus Christ, then I'm waiting on the wrong things. You have some people who are waiting for a whole bunch of money to just drop out of the sky, or waiting for a luxury car, or a big house.

Who is your master? If Jesus Christ is my master, then that means I'm waiting on Jesus. This means that if Jesus knows what I want and I'm waiting on Jesus, then I'm not going to settle for the second best. I told God the exact kind of woman I like, so when something comes that's similar, but she's not exactly what I asked for, then it is the wrong person.

When you're waiting on God, God is going to give you precisely what you asked for. We don't serve a God who will give you half of what you ask for. That's not what my pastor taught me. He said, "He will give you the desires of your heart if you delight yourself in The Word. If My Word abide in you and you abide in My Word, you shall ask and it shall be given. But that's with a condition. "If you abide in my word and my word abide in you."

(sermon continued on page 171)

ELEVEN

Pastor Jonathan Carter

I took a deep breath. I swallowed as I adjusted my notes.
"God is not pleased" was how I began my very first sermon.
I talked about relationships—with man and with God. I told
the congregation that the same things you want out of a relationship with your man or woman—faithfulness, honesty,
trust, loyalty, unconditional love—are the very things God
wants from you.

"No one wants a companion who hangs out all the time
with people who don't like them," I said. "God doesn't want
you hanging with people who don't like Him, either. You
don't want somebody who lies. Neither does God. You want a
man or a woman who loves you no matter what—fat, skinny,
old or young, through good and bad times. God wants unconditional love, too.

"With your man, you are willing to try stuff once—even

stuff you know ain't good for you. No questions asked. But when it comes to God, you need an explanation."

There were so many people sitting there in the congregation, and I was as surprised as I could see they were. Throughout the message the people were attentive. When I was done my pastor was convinced that God was going to use me to lead a lot of people to the Kingdom."

He was telling to me to stay focused. Pastor Jonathan Carter always gave me good advice.

Pastor Carter and Siloam wasn't the first church I stumbled upon.

After searching for a church for months, visiting different ministries and listening to different pastors, I found Siloam Baptist Church. It was totally God leading me there.

I was driving to get something to eat with a pastor whose church I had been attending. And while we were at the light, a man pulled up next to us in a van. On the side of this van were the words SILOAM BAPTIST CHURCH. I didn't think it was a coincidence. I operate on faith. For me, that was enough.

As much as I've been through, I know that it was nothing but God's grace and mercy that has brought me this far. And if you can believe that out of all the stuff I've done that God still wants to use me, then I had to know He would lead me to where He wanted me to be.

I called the number—I had remembered it from the van that day—and a lady answered. She said her name was Sister Mason.

This must be the place for me.

I found the church, which was on Holcomb Avenue in East Atlanta, during the week and met with the pastor, Jonathan Carter. He treated me—with love—like he would treat anyone else off the street. He didn't know me as anything but a young man seeking the Lord. I guess he didn't listen to much rap back at home in Valley, Alabama.

We started talking, and I was telling Pastor Carter that I needed to know God.

So I started going to Siloam every Sunday. After the first Sunday service, the youth leaders at that time were telling me all the classes I had to finish before I could officially be an active member of the church. But then there were some little kids asking me for an autograph. If I'm going to classes like everybody else, then I can't give out autographs.

I can't be regular and a celebrity at the same time.

"Either y'all are gonna make me a celebrity or treat me like a regular person all the time," I said to them. And the autograph-seeking stopped. But eventually more and more people started coming to Siloam every Sunday. Some people came to see if Ma$e was serious, and ended up seeing Christ move through Pastor Jonathan Carter. Every Sunday he carries the anointing. And most of those people who may have initially come to see what was up with Ma$e, ended up becoming permanent members of Siloam. Praise God. That's how good He works.

I came to Siloam just looking for any kind of help. Pastor Carter ended up being more help than I thought I needed. He nurtured me; he took me in as a son. I could call him and pray with him all the time. It was hard for him to get rid of me and as a result I stayed away from my old habits—some not so easily, but eventually they all went away.

I wasn't having sex; I wasn't drinking or smoking weed anymore. It was easy because I was around Pastor Carter and he definitely wasn't doing any of those things.

When those old urges tried to come back, I would stay around him. We became so tight that I would say to him "Pastor, God is . . ." and he would finish the sentence. He knew what I was thinking and the things I was struggling with.

I knew when I came to the Lord, I needed a teacher, someone to show me the way. I knew I had to go somewhere, sit down, and let somebody teach me. I was willing to do anything to learn, to the point of being a servant to the man of God.

The Bible says, whoever wants to be great among you, let him first serve. I was an untitled assistant to Pastor Carter, and I learned from serving.

Pastor Carter gave me my training wheels and kept my bike straight until I could do it by myself. Then he took off the training wheels when he felt I didn't need them and gave me advice on how to ride. This was better for me than having someone steering the bike for me, with me riding on the handlebars. Then I would feel that I always needed that person to steer my way for me, and I would never learn how to ride for myself.

My pastor was the one. The one who, when I went there asking questions, opened the Bible, showed me the answers, and taught me how to find the answers for myself. I went to Tuesday afternoon Bible study classes. And he took me to every revival that he preached. I mean, we were going to some backwoods churches and churches that were held in people's houses.

My pastor gave me books to study—more books than I ever read in school. Everything I would read in the Bible, I would get a life test on it that day.

I had to learn so I wouldn't be out there being bold and ignorant. My pastor taught me everything that he experienced and everything to look out for—which was a lot considering he had been preaching since he was fifteen.

He also taught me that I wasn't to teach what I believed or what I felt. "Teach exactly what Christ says." He showed me how to live righteously and he informed me of what God expects of me. He took me through a lot of teachings on demonic spirits that come after you as a man of God.

"You have such a strong ministry that the last thing the enemy will want to do is make it easy for you to succeed," he told me. "Your ministry will set some captives free that some ministers couldn't reach." He told me to always remember that it's not about me. It's all God's doing.

"Three things I want you to remember, son," he said. "Number one: It's not about you. Number two: God is in control. Number three: Count it all joy." He said when bad things happen, count it all joy because it's actually working for you.

What I love about Pastor Carter is that he is always sincere and operates with integrity. He didn't know nothing about the world I came from. And that was good. In his eyes, it was just sin. He never treated me special. And by the time he learned who Ma$e really was, it was too late. Ma$e was gone. And Mason was already a minister.

God sent me to Siloam and it worked out great for both of us.

To this day, I still try to attend his Bible classes every Tuesday and I go to keep learning. You don't ever stop learning the Word of God. Before I had my own ministry, I would go every day. So I'm still consistent.

For a whole year all I did was work out and study the Word. I had to keep myself in shape. When people come to know the Lord, many of them couldn't care less about how they look. They get so caught up in God that they neglect the temple God gave them—their own body. I caught them vapors at first. I wouldn't cut my hair and was getting this afro. I was getting skinny, too. But I realized I had to take care of His temple the way I was taking care of His Word.

God was showing me He wanted me to be balanced. I started to get into a schedule. I would wake up at 6 A.M. and pray. Eat at 7 A.M., work out from 8 to 10 A.M., shower and get dressed from 10 to 11, straighten up the house, eat lunch, go to the library from 1 to 3 P.M., shoot hoops after that, and then go to church. Every day I was in church, every morning I would pray, every afternoon I would play ball.

I was at a place where God saw I was sincere. I started going to school at Clark University in Atlanta. And I started enjoying Bible study at the school with some of the students. We would read a chapter in the Bible every day and examine it as a group. One time, an entertainer came to Clark to do a radio promo for his album. The school was so big that they had the radio show outside. He saw me on campus and we ended up talking.

He said, "There's some fine girls in here, I know you be having fun."

I said, "Nah, I'm not into that anymore." And I showed him the Bible.

And he said, "I can respect that," and walked away. I know that's going to stick in his mind.

When I first started studying with Pastor Carter, I would come home and cry because I didn't understand the Bible and I wanted to know more and more. I was so used to mastering stuff quickly. I couldn't understand why I couldn't get this. The Bible says if any man wants wisdom, let him ask. I was asking and still not getting any more wisdom. My problem was I was trying too hard to understand the way of the Lord. You have to understand that you will not always understand God. That's the only way you and God can have a good understanding.

I had faith. And now I understand the Word. And I thank Pastor Carter for being my teacher. Everyone needs a teacher, and every teacher needs a student to carry on his legacy and do even greater things.

Moses had Joshua. David had Solomon. Jesus had the twelve disciples. Paul had Timothy. Pastor Carter has Mason. And the list goes on.

So when they had dined, Jesus saith to Simon Peter, Simon son of Jō´nas, lovest thou me more than these? He saith unto him, Yea, Lord; thou knowest that I love thee. He saith unto him, Feed my lambs.

—John 21:15

Sermon

I waiteth on the Lord. I'm not waiteth on Puff Daddy. I'm not waiteth on Magic Johnson. I'm not waiteth on my pastor. I'm not waiteth on the ministers, I'm not waiteth on my brother, I'm not waiteth on my mother, I'm not waiteth on a degree, I'm not waiteth on no woman, I'm not waiteth on no choir, I'm not waiteth on nobody but Jesus, because that's who my strength comes from. The moment nobody's waiting on the Lord then I'm not going to wait on somebody who's not waiting on the Lord.

Waiteth. Now this is something that has conditions. The Bible says, Whoso that keepeth the fig tree shall eat the fruit thereof. *Conditions. This means if I can't keepeth the fig tree, then when the fruit comes, don't be trying to eat it. You have your people who leave the tree when there's nothing growing on it. Then when the tree starts flourishing, they want to come back. If you're going to be down, be down.*

One thing about me, when I gave my life to Christ, I became a fig tree. People just vanished out of nowhere. I just looked around and said, "Oh my goodness, I'm by myself. Where is everybody at? Where are all of the people who I gave money to pay their rent? Where are all the people I personally took care of?

I ended up with a person standing by me who I never even had a solid relationship with—my brother. Never. My brother was the one who went to jail. He did a lot of bad things. Everybody said he's not going to be anything. You don't need to be with him. But my brother is one who is saved with me now.

I would just say, "Yo, Mike, God's been telling me to leave rap and I'm going to Atlanta. Are you coming? We don't know where the next check is coming from, but are you coming? We ain't got no more videos to do. But are you coming? We ain't got no more radio appearances, no more autograph signings, no more nothing. But are you coming? I ain't got no more women to offer you, I ain't got no more weed to offer you, but are you coming? I can't get you in nothing VIP no more, but are you coming?"

My brother is the one when I first brought him to church who would storm out. And I would be like, "God, what are you trying to tell me?" But now my brother is saved. My brother is baptized. Because he was willing to keepeth the fig tree, so now when the fruit comes, he's the first to eat. He believed when there was nothing.

(sermon continued on page 185)

TWELVE

S.A.N.E. Ministries

After spending two years under Pastor Carter—and I was comfortable being under him, learning from him—God was ready for me to move.

Maybe I was becoming too comfortable. When that happens, you tend to slack off and lay back. When you're comfortable, you don't work as hard.

Pastor Carter and Siloam Baptist Church have sheltered me enough.

I had to talk to my pastor. I wanted the blessings of the man of God I was studying under. I wanted it to be in decency and in order. I didn't want Pastor Carter to think that I got everything I could from him and now and I'm ready to leave.

I believed that if it was the right time, God would tell him also. I wanted to be sure.

I prayed, "Lord, let your will be done."

I went to speak with my pastor about what was in my heart, and before I could get my words out he said, "Mason, I think it's time for you to branch out. We've done our part. It's

173

time for you to pursue what God has for you. For me to keep you at this church would be selfish."

I knew what God was telling me to do. I knew the type of ministry He wanted me to have. But I didn't know where to start it or what steps God wanted me to take. We prayed about it.

I met with the pastor's wife, Sister Sylvia Carter, and she told me she was praying for me. And she encouraged me by telling me: "He's going to use you to help save a nation of people. He wants you to know that everything you've done for the devil, he's going to use for Himself [and she didn't mean rapping]. He's going to place the right people in your life and they're not going to use you."

She told me God gave her a vision of my ministry.

"It was S.A.N.E. Ministries," she said. "That stands for 'Saving a Nation.' But I couldn't come up with the 'E'." Then she let me know that I had to come up with what the 'E' meant."

At first, I had no idea what she was talking about. But I said, "Since it came from the Word, let's go to the Word."

And we opened up the concordance in the back of the Bible and the first "E" word we came to was "endangered." I went and studied that word and it said, "It's a danger that's already in them." Meaning the danger is present, the sin is in them.

These were the people that nobody thought could be saved. But God was telling me that because of the cries of His people I've been called to lead them back to Him.

I could see it. It was for me, Mason Betha, to go back to every place where Ma$e once was and help the people to know Christ. I had to tell them to "Repent, for the Kingdom of God is at hand," and "Hell is not full." And I was thinking if God takes me everywhere that Ma$e once was so the people can see the CHRIST in Mason Betha, that would be a movement in and of itself.

My pastor and I sat down and I told him about a fifty-city crusade to kick off S.A.N.E. Ministries. We picked fifty cities where Ma$e toured. Our first stop was Dallas, Texas.

When Ma$e was in Texas, everything was sold out. People couldn't wait to get their tickets. They would call the radio stations, fighting for free tickets. Everyone went out and bought their best outfits and really didn't care how much the concert was. It would cost a hundred dollars to be in the front row and about twenty dollars to be in the nosebleed seats. People found a way to be there, young and old. And when the concert would be over, the people would leave as empty as they came—not feeding their mind, body, or soul.

When I came to town as Mason, I promoted the crusade in a similar way you would promote a concert because that was the only way I knew. I went on radio stations. We had flyers handed out in the streets. I didn't go into anybody's church to promote it because I didn't want to have it in a church. We had to go to the streets where the majority of Ma$e's audience was. I want to grab up those same people and give them the food of Life I never could have given them as Ma$e.

The people Christ wanted to reach through me, for the most part, couldn't be found in churches. These people may feel they've done too much wrong to go into a church. So we had it at PC Cobb, which held about two thousand people.

Before I came out to speak I was on fire. I was ready. This was the first time I was speaking to an audience who only knew me as Ma$e, and did I have a message for them. I came out onstage and there was silence. And emptiness. There were maybe four hundred people in this two-thousand-seat gymnasium and it seemed like every person was on the edge of their seat waiting to hear the first words to come out of my mouth, waiting to see how I would respond to the turnout.

"Ma$e would have sold out this joint ten times," is what Satan whispered. "They would have had to move it to an arena. Why aren't they screaming and hollering? You're nothing. This is all just one big joke."

That was rough.

I blocked out Satan and this Scripture came to me: "What the Lord loves, the world hates."

Those were the first words out of my mouth. I guess I shouldn't have expected a lot of people in the world to show up. They were in that mode where, "It's just Ma$e; it's a publicity stunt."

But the people who were there really needed the message I presented that day, which was "Hell is not full." But by the looks on their faces, they didn't want that message. They didn't want Mason. They wanted Ma$e. And that was the first time that I knew for sure that none of those people made me. And I became even more fired up to preach.

I started really getting into the message. And the more passionate I became, the more obstacles seemed to come up. The sound system was acting funny. There was a choir that was supposed to sing and for no apparent reason decided they couldn't sing.

But I didn't let Satan's ploy stop me.

When people see you work through obstacles it just makes

more people get saved. They're used to seeing people go through things and give up. But here I was with no crowd, no mic, no choir, and I was still preaching.

By the time God was finished, if there were four hundred people in that auditorium, three hundred were at the altar. When I was finished, every person in there knew that God did His thing. And what the people gave in their offering was enough or as much as it would have been if the place was packed. God was showing me to not get caught up in numbers, that He will work no matter how many people show up.

Sure, Ma$e would have sold it out because Ma$e was working for the devil. We're in a generation where people got to see it. They go off of rep. God was building me up for something bigger. He wanted me to be a man not caught up in people or in numbers or money. With him knowing I came from music and was used to making millions and used to seeing crowds, he wanted to make sure that appetite was gone. He wanted me to be able to appreciate where he was taking me.

As I said earlier, when I announced to my church that I was getting married, half the people left. But God showed me that, even without all of those people, we would carry on. You think we don't have enough? We do. Even without all those people, we have not missed a beat. I haven't missed a bill or a meal. God is faithful to those who are faithful to Him.

He showed me that numbers don't matter, impact does. I'm into quality, not quantity. There's nothing wrong with having quantity, ain't nothing wrong with having a big church. I just don't want a hundred people if only thirty are going to fight this fight. Then just give me those thirty. At least I know what I'm working with.

I can't lie. At first I was a little worried and concerned. But God is so awesome that you don't have to compromise. You can stand solely on the Word. Now when I go out, the places are packed. Some days I wake up and it's so amazing. Everything I would have made with music, I have with God. That melts my heart.

I recently called my accountant and told him I wanted to close all my accounts. I told him to send every penny that Ma$e made to S.A.N.E. Ministries' account. We're going to build God's Kingdom off of the wealth of the wicked. And I'm going to start my life off anew.

I'm not going out there and building a big church with lots of fancy stained glass and pretty walls and floors, and chandeliers and other stuff like that. Right now, we hold services in a school auditorium and it's come as you are. Wherever you are, however you look, whatever your circumstances, you're welcome.

My church is God's church. He's placed me over it. In our church we have intercessory. We pray for the lost people and people struggling. We're a loving and for-real church. This is a warfare church. A church that believes in missions and missionaries—that believes in going out and bringing people in to be empowered.

Every Sunday we open the service for God to do something new. Some Sundays we may praise God all service. Another Sunday we just do the offering. Some Sundays there is just the Word. You can never tell what's going to happen, that's why you can't afford to miss one Sunday.

Some days people may get healed. And that's real exciting because there are young people who need to see these types of miracles take place. I'm just a vehicle to display God's greatness. There were some days I felt like I was being watched so much that God couldn't let me fall.

I was recently on a crusade through some major cities like New York City and Los Angeles—cities where Ma$e was a big influence as a rapper. God told me to ask people for a certain amount and I would never do it.

"I can't ask people for money," I said to God. "The last time they saw me I was a millionaire." When they saw me I was a big baller and I didn't want them to think I was struggling. But that was ego. And pride.

God humbled me. Things weren't working out and the ministry was not being blessed.

That's why we had to start out in a school—because if I had done what God had told me to do, we would have had a church. But God, knowing my heart, still blessed us. It's not about big churches and how we look to the world. But God wanted me to know that I wouldn't have these big headaches if I did what He said.

"I placed you in those cities for you to be a blessing to the people and for the people to bless you. And you wouldn't ask them," God said.

And God took me on a long journey and let me struggle for real. And I learned my lesson. Ever since then, we've been getting miraculous blessings. I don't even know who is sending the money most of the time, they just send it. That is God.

I went to Los Angeles and God told me to call certain celebrities. I couldn't understand why they wouldn't help and why they wouldn't respond. This showed me that He wanted to keep me humble. First, God wanted me to know it was Him doing it.

We need to get SANE.

These young kids out here can sense what's real. We want to know why they don't want to go to church. You can hand your baby to somebody and your baby won't go to certain people. How does a baby know who they should go to and who they shouldn't be going to? Babies are pure. They don't know everything, but they know when something's not right. They can feel it. They're not tainted.

You want to be effective with young people? Teach them how to fight this spiritual war. Stop compromising the gospel. Take a stand. Live it. Stop trying to manipulate the gospel to get them to come to church. They don't respect that. They look at you as being weak because you're bending what you know to be right hoping it will lead them to Christ. You can't use devilish ways to bring these kids to God.

I know these young people can get saved. I know these people can be saved. I know not just because God told me, but because I'm living proof. Some days I cry because I realize how lost I was and God still saved me.

God is awesome.

My next step is to build an army—an army that will send a blow to the devil's camp that he's never heard before. These will have to be soldiers who are willing to die for trusting in the Lord—where we take it by force, by the power of God. Everything we've been through, it's time to strike back. How much do we let the devil do to us, and we never do anything back? As much as we complain about the devil having our family members, what do we do about it? Don't you want to get some of those souls back?

I don't know about you, but I'm tired of him.

If he hits my family, I'm going to make sure more families come to Christ. If he attacks my church and disturbs us, I'm going to disturb the clubs. If he attacks my people, I will make sure his people get attacked. (I'm going to do that anyway by making sure we keep the gospel ever before them.)

When Satan does something, there are repercussions. Satan is a bully. He goes where he knows he can do something and get away with it. He attacks the best of the saints but when they submit to God and resist him, he has to flee.

What keeps me going is when I think about how many people he's got of mine. I can't give in to him. No matter how much my flesh may want it, I can't give in. I got friends and family, people I still need to see get saved. When I think of how many years he had me in darkness—where I didn't know the truth—I couldn't live with knowing that all the people I know who are still in darkness will not be delivered.

I feel like my whole life is in a witness-protection program. It's like I went against the mob and I have to stay away from people who will turn me in. In that world you can't even trust family members because anybody can turn you in.

I've turned in state's evidence on the devil and I'm now testifying against him. I'm speaking against the very things that could endanger my life. I know he's not going to sit by and allow me to keep doing it without trying to do something to me or my family. But I'm willing to take that chance. I'm sold out for Jesus. Are you?

But they that will be rich fall into temptation and a snare, and into *many foolish and hurtful lusts, which drown men in destruction and perdition.*

For the love of money is the root of all evil: which while some coveted after, they have erred from the faith, and pierced themselves through with many sorrows.

— 1 Timothy 6:9-10

Sermon

We kept the fig tree. It might not have been the fig tree everybody else wanted us to be, but we kept the fig tree. Now it's time to eat the fruit thereof. One thing these conditions offer us is the willingness to be patient. It also gives us wisdom. God can give wisdom to a young man. Jesus was twelve years old when he first came to understand the wisdom of the Bible. He started his ministry when he was thirty-three.

When God called Jesus, He gave him the wisdom. He gave Him patience to be able to deal with misguided people. As a great leader, one is going to need patience and wisdom. When you're a fig tree, you don't have nothing so you have to be patient and waiteth.

I wanted God to make me a wise man. I was like Solomon—I didn't really want the money and all of that stuff. I just wanted to be wise. People would say, "But you're so smart." I didn't want to be smart, I wanted to be wise. There's a difference between a smart man and a wise man. A smart man finds clever ways to do things. A smart man has all of these new ideas and ways to do things— always has fresh ideas. A wise man knows how to do intellectual things, knows how to do the right things, knows how to come up with the clever ideas. But the key to a wise man is he knows what to do when all those things don't work. See, a smart man doesn't know that. He's too smart and crafty for his own good.

I'd rather be a wise man with patience while I'm a fig tree. When the fruit comes, I'll be wise enough to know what to do with the fruit. See, you eat the fruit but there is still a seed in there. So when I'm bearing fruit—the fruit has seeds and those seeds are going to bring even more fruit. As a flourishing tree, I shouldn't be just getting people saved. I should be getting people saved who are getting people saved.

We're still on the topic, "Hell is never full," but I have to give you this background information so that you can fully understand what I'm saying when I say, "Hell is never full."

(sermon continued on page 195)

THIRTEEN

The Root of All Evil

Money. Some people got to have it. Some people think they really need it. I used to think I needed it. But with money comes so many problems. Money just brings a whole other aspect to the table that nothing else can. Money brings aggression. Because of money I had to drive around Manhattan for twenty minutes before I would be going home to Secaucus, New Jersey, to make sure I wasn't being followed.

Money made guns my protection. I didn't want to be seen with a bunch of bodyguards—that would make me look like a punk. So while I hated guns, money made me feel I needed one—just in case. Money had me leery of death because I knew I was wearing enough jewelry to get me killed.

I always felt that the moment you become successful, nothing else matters. Life becomes so easy. When you have money, when you're a celebrity, no one cares about your color or gender. Money don't matter when you have it. They give you everything free—free clothes, free cars, free shoes, and more opportunities to make money. When you have money you get into places for free, you get to eat for free, drink for free. When you're broke, you pay for everything. It's really backward.

Less fortunate people end up going broke, spending their money on things rich people get for free.

When I didn't have money I was cool with everybody. Maybe it was because we were all broke, therefore we were all on the same page. The moment I received the money, nobody looked at me like Mason no more. It was Ma$e. M-A-$-E. Mason no longer existed in people's eyes. The women saw Ma$e. Sad to say, even my friends began to call me Ma$e.

Even my name was about money. When I started rapping there was already a Mase with De La Soul. So I changed mine to M-A-$-E. I got the idea from the cartoon Richie Rich and how the Cs were cent signs. I wanted the world to know I was going to make dollars. Looking back, how stupid was I?

Once I got the money I couldn't care less about people. I was on guard—expecting them to try and take something from me. I was beginning to think people were only around me for money. So eventually, I didn't care how I treated people because to me they were only around for the money.

After a while it became, "It's the game, get used to it." I figured so many punches come to you that you either hit or be hit, snake or be snaked. It was no better than the drug game.

Instead of selling coke, you'd be selling albums, selling souls. Instead of snitching, you were gossiping. Instead of going to jail, you just fell off the map. The music game is a crime and all the money that comes with it is blood money.

They say that money is the root of all evil. You hear that all the time. But it's the *love* of money that is the root of all evil. Actually, it's the love of anything outside of God that is the root of all evil. It's impossible to love riches and try to love God. The Bible says you cannot serve two masters. Either you will hate the one and love the other. You cannot serve both God and mammon.

That doesn't mean you cannot be rich. You can have the money and not love it. You can also have money and let the money have you.

Keeping up with the Joneses is the love of money. If you always have to do what everybody else is doing or buy what the next man has—even if you don't have it like that—that's wrong.

I used to buy things I didn't need just to be flossing. But that was ignorant and childish. Now that I am a man, I had to put away my childish things.

You could have money for a Rolls-Royce, but that don't mean you have to buy one. If the things you want stop you from becoming the kind of person God wants you to be, God doesn't want you to have them.

Why live in a way that's going to kill you? Why drive a hundred thousand dollar car and still live with your mother or in the projects? Diamonds everywhere, dripping in platinum and you don't have a house that's paid for—that's not

God's vision. If your car is worth more than your house, that's backward.

We have to wisely spend the money God gives us. That's what I did.

If you love money you're going to use people. If you love people, you could use the money to show you love them.

I bought my first house in Florida, and it felt so good to be responsible and put my money into something practical that wasn't a waste—something that increases with value over time instead of like a car, which depreciates as soon as you drive it off the lot.

It was a great feeling. It's everybody's dream to tell their mother, "Pack up! We're moving!" Mine didn't come at a good time.

I got a special pleasure from buying my mother a house. At the time I couldn't really afford to buy her the house of her dreams but I made a sacrifice.

One day my mother sat us down and told us that she wanted to be buried in Florida, in her hometown. I never wanted her to wait until she died to go home. So I took her to Florida and told her to look for the house she wanted. "Maybe one day we'll be able to get it," I said.

She found a house she really liked and we came back to New York. The next week I gave her the keys and said, "You might as well tell Luck [Samuel's nickname] to pack your stuff. You're moving!"

She was so happy. The look on her face was a Kodak moment. She has a beautiful house with gates and a Rottweiler that runs around the yard all night. As many hard times as she had—some of which I contributed to—in life she deserved to enjoy every bit of that house. Parents sometimes feel like a failure when none of their kids do anything productive.

I don't love money. But I will use money. Money isn't evil. But once it's loved by the people, it becomes a very wicked thing. And as much as you would love to have money, money would love to have you.

I can do all these things through Christ which strengtheneth me.

—PHILLIPPIANS 4:13

Blessed are *the pure of heart: for they shall see God.*

—MATTHEW 5:8

Sermon

A person could confess with their mouth that they're saved and
not be sanctified. Sanctified means to separate. When you
become sanctified that means God is separating you, you're really
letting God come into your life. When you're a fig tree, you are by
yourself—separate, sanctified. When you're by yourself and you
have nothing, that is usually when people allow God to do what He
can do. If He gives you all the fruit before you know what it is like
to be a fig tree, then you probably wouldn't stay sanctified. But now
that He's keeping you lonely and keeping you by yourself, when you
get the fruit you'll know—when I was a fig tree I was by myself so I
don't need to get something from God and then become unlike a fig
tree. As a man of God I realize I'm not going to be with a lot of
people. Even when God blesses me and starts doing all these mighty
things for me that my pastor and everybody else keeps prophesying,
I'm still going to have to be a fig tree. If not, then the monkeys and
the owls and everything else are going to destroy my tree.

Being sanctified and as a fig tree, God has allowed me to grow
and have more faith in Him. Had he not separated you and kept
you lonely, then you wouldn't totally depend on Him. Now you
might be thinking, "Why did God make him a fig tree?" This is
only a parable from the Bible—a fig tree. There's no man named

fig tree. This is a parable because God is omniscient, God is all-knowing. He knew what He had to do in order for you to believe in the Scripture. He used the parable of a fig tree because a fig tree symbolizes standing alone. There are a lot of people who will have to stand alone. You have kids who don't have parents, so they have to stand alone. You have some parents who are no help to their kids, so in essence these children stand alone. Then you have kids who are rebellious to their parents and the parents basically have to stand alone and pray that God will work out the situation. God also used the parable because He knows people don't like to be alone.

You have to ask yourself, "Why don't I like to be alone?" You will learn more about yourself (if you're alone). But Satan doesn't want you to learn more about yourself because Hell and destruction is never full.

Hell and destruction are never full, so the eyes of men are never satisfied. *Never satisfied. When I look back on my life, it lets me know why I should be satisfied. I was only in music so I could get a name so God could use that name. I was only in school to learn how to study, just to be able to study the Word. I was only trying to be obedient because God wanted me to be obedient to show other young people you can have material things, you can be popular and you can still be obedient. Looking back on my life, all of that makes sense.*

(sermon continued on page 203)

FOURTEEN

Steps to Staying Faithful

Only the righteous will see God. How does a person become righteous? By practicing. How do you become good at anything? Practice.

I'm a person who will always study. I want to become a master of God's Word. I study every day. Some days I just read. Some days I may write a sermon. Every day, I pray, but some days I listen to what God has to say.

You must set aside time to listen to what God has to say. Many times when we pray, we're basically telling God what we want. When was the last time you sat down and said to God, "What is it that You desire for my life?"

When I asked God what He will have me to do, that was the best experience of my life. I started getting better results and quicker results. When God speaks, it's so clear. When you listen to Him, He sends you to all the right places to help you avoid confusion. It's not always easy. Sometimes God doesn't speak. But by knowing God's Word you know God well enough to know His answers."

Below are a few things that have kept me faithful and on the path to righteousness.

1. Watch God and Not Man

If you watch people, chances are you're going to quit. That's the biggest mistake made by many Christians, new and old. They watch what the next person is doing. Most times, this is the very thing that discourages people from coming to church. If you see someone is sinning or doing wrong, that doesn't give you a license to do wrong, even if it's your pastor. If you're living right, no one man has a greater chance of getting into heaven than you do. In fact, it's harder for a prophet because on Judgment Day, God will hold prophets doubly accountable. Remember, God sees all and that's who you should be living to please—not man.

Just know that we are all operating under God's grace while trying to get to heaven. Grace is a favor you can't work for. Grace is you waking up in the morning—you didn't do anything special to make sure you woke up. That's just God's grace. So, keep your eyes on the Lord. I repeat, keep your eyes on the Lord. Jesus is the role model. Jesus is the standard.

2. Count It All Joy

No matter how bad it is, count it all joy. Even when they're plotting against you, be happy. Because it's going to end up working in your favor. In Scripture it says, "No weapon formed against me can prosper." That's so true. When you are walking in the light and your life is established in righteousness, nothing can harm you. But don't forget, this promise is only for those who have kept His Commandments. Commandment keepers don't have to worry about bad times, they just have to live by faith. And trust that all of the bad taking place will be turned around for God's glory. And their enemies, the very trap they set, may be their own.

The reason why I count it all joy is because I know God sometimes uses trouble to prepare you. Every trial I've been through has led to a blessing either for myself or somebody else. Every hardship I've faced was used to help someone else know God. And that's a real blessing.

When you can take the bitter things and turn them into a sweet situation, you have overcome. When you can take your lemons of life and squeeze them into lemonade, maybe somebody else's thirst can be quenched. There's no reason to sit around and wallow in their sorrows. Why wrap yourself in the scars and feel sorry for yourself? Feeling sorry for yourself is not going to change the situation. Count it all joy. Nobody can steal that.

3. It's Not About You

Everybody wants to do what they want to do. Everybody wants to do what they feel. But it's about what God wants to do through you. There's a purpose that God has for every person—a path that only God can reveal. It boils down to this: Do you want to surrender to it? I don't think anybody wants to intentionally be lost. But when they walk or follow their own desires, they often miss the road God has for them. Then they end up walking around wanting everything God has for them and then have the nerve to go back to God and say, "Why are things not working out for me?"

Things can't go right if you're not right. Especially if you're doing your plan, not God's. I had to realize this myself. I had to come to the conclusion that it's not about me at all. It's all about who God wants to bless through me.

People want to know how a person can do something wrong and have God still bless them and use them. Because God is a God of grace and mercy and you can't question His plan. The gift is not for that person—it's for God to use. And when it's used, it's to help God's people. And as long as God gets the glory, that's all that matters. It's not about me or you.

4. GOD IS IN CONTROL

This last point kind of sums up all the others. God is in control: If people can get this in their minds and in their hearts, they wouldn't worry so much and be anxious. People can't sleep. They're always on pins and needles. Why? I don't worry. Even the Bible says that we should not worry. "So do not worry saying, 'What shall we eat?' or 'What shall we drink?' or 'What shall we wear?' For the pagans run after these things, and your heavenly Father knows that you need them. Seek first His Kingdom and His righteousness and these things will be given to you as well."

So if God knows you need it and you trust that God can do it, why worry?

I haven't always been a person who didn't worry. But now I don't worry about anything. I'm in a season now where I'm beginning to get everything back, like Job. He lost everything, his family, his property, his livestock, his friends—and in the end God gave him back everything tenfold.

I tried living my life on my will, in my way, and I was unhappy and insane.

Now I trust that God is God. God is in control.

Sermon

I'm now standing before you as a fig tree. Eventually I shall get my fruit. Even when this happens, there will be people who will criticize me. You will have to ask yourself, Why would a person criticize a man who's going to get my daughter saved? Why would I criticize the young man who's going to make my son come home? Why would I criticize the young man who's going to help everything I'm trying to do happen more freely?

God works through people. Isn't it ironic that everything I'm praying for is right in front of me? You—young people. Many people are scared to use young people. They're going to go to hell anyway if they die young, so why not use them while they are young? There's no reason to say, "Well, he's that age, so we're going to sit him down." No. Use him. When you use him, that's going to open the window for all of those blessings to come.

Hell and destruction are never full. So the eyes of men are never satisfied. *In order for you to properly understand this sermon, I have to break down two words—eye and full. What is an eye? Eyes represent vision. An eye is insight. An eye is what God gave us, not just to see, but also to watch. The eye is sight. In thinking about the word full, enough, plenty comes to mind. Full means it's full, we're not letting anymore people in. If the glass is full, don't throw more ice into it because it will overflow.*

The Bible says Hell and destruction are never full. *Hell has more space, more room.* Hell and destruction are never full. *Hell is not already full, as some may imagine? As much evil as we see going on, hell is still not full? As many young people killing each other, lying on each other, sleeping with each other, hell ain't full? As many of my friends died in the streets, you mean to tell me hell is not full? As many people died selling drugs, hell is not full? As many people died in the church being hypocrites, hell is not full? And when hell is not full, that means you can look forward to more people going.*

The two words I'm on are "eye" and "full." Now I'm going to put them together—eyeful. You have a lot of people getting an "eyeful" of the wrong things. Eyeful. My help cometh from the North—not the East and the West. So where am I looking? North. I got an eyeful of the North. I got an eyeful of heaven, I got an eyeful of the Holy Spirit. I got an eyeful of angels. I got an eyeful of the anointing. I got an eyeful of Jesus. An eyeful. What do you get an eyeful of today when you examine our society?

The eye sees lust and lust becomes desire and desire becomes sin and sin becomes carnal and carnal becomes death. But it all started with an eye, an eyeful. I could get an eyeful of the wrong woman. I could get an eyeful of the wrong magazine. I could get an eyeful of the wrong videotape. I could get an eyeful of the wrong things. An eyeful.

Now if my help cometh from the North, where should I be looking? If I got an eyeful and I'm one of the strong, one of the irons, one of the Christians, the sharp, the sword, the little razors, the little box cutter, then I'm looking to get an eyeful of Jesus. The reason people can't get an eyeful of Jesus is because they're not looking North.

An eyeful. If I'm not looking North, where can I be looking? South. What's South? Hell. That's why hell is never full. If I'm not looking North and say, "Okay, I ain't looking North and I ain't looking South." You have some people who say they ain't looking North and I ain't looking South. I'm not focusing on God and I'm not focusing on Satan, either. Where are you looking? East and West. So you watching everybody else, huh? You're getting an eyeful of everybody else.

If I can offer anything to young people, it is hell and destruction are never full. Don't let Satan use you. Because just like the young people don't like the old people to be judging them. Don't be judging old people. You don't want them judging you because you're new and you got new ways of doing things. Don't judge them for being traditional. So it works both ways. Just like they need to learn how to find new routines, you need to learn a little bit about tradition. You need to know about what you don't want to be like.

As a new believer I began by looking East and West. I wasn't looking at God and I wasn't looking at Satan. I can talk about this because God has delivered me from it. When I first came to church, I used to just watch the pulpit. I would say, I ain't going to this church because the pastor returned to the pulpit after they took the offering or any other lame reason. I was judging because I was looking East and West. When you look North, you don't judge anyone but yourself as you try to live by The Word.

When I really think about everything that God has done, I realize He has called on me to be a waiter. All men of God—don't look at them as perfect—are waiters. Women of God are waitresses. This means, we don't need to look East and West, worrying about money and other material and superficial things. As a servant of God, if I serve good food, I'm going to get a big tip. I'm serving nothing but good food and I'm serving it with kindness, with love. One thing you've got to know about a waiter, as a pastor, as a minister, my life is designed to study and prepare your food every moment of my life. Do you really want to talk about the man who is preparing your food? Do you know what happens when you talk about people who are preparing your food? You end up with something in your food that sets you straight. You shouldn't talk about the men of God. Never ever, ever, ever talk about the men of God, the women of God, the preachers of God, the singers of God, the ushers of God, the choirs of God, the musicians of God. You end up with something in your food that was not meant for you.

While you're looking East and West, keep in mind that it ain't South. You still need to look North. When you don't believe in Satan and you don't believe in God, you don't know why you do what you do. There's only two reasons any man does wrong. Only two. In the whole Bible there are only two reasons: Either Satan is using you, or hell is not full. When you get to a point when you're reading the wrong things, watching the wrong programs, listening to the wrong radio stations, it is because hell is not full. Satan is still recruiting. When you are talking about people negatively and you don't know the reason, it is because Satan is using you. Hell is not full.

When you're doing anything and God is not getting the glory out of it, who is using you? If what you're doing ain't getting a shout, who is using you? When you say, I just have to do this— smoke this weed, have this drink, sleep with someone—*who's using you?* How about when you say, I need more time to get myself together. *Who told you that?*

When your sole purpose involves saving, Heaven, glory, angels, trumpets, violins, piano, cheerfulness, happiness, love, peace, wisdom, annointing, power, authority, glory, victory, Jesus, God, Heaven, pearly gates, Elohim, and Jehovah Jirah, then God is using you.

If I'm miserable, unhappy, feeling unwanted, bitter, angry, anxious, deceitful, backstabbing, lying, conniving, perverted, adulterous, stealing, robbing, murdering, raping, addicted to drugs and alcohol, ignorant, not fathering my kids, not mothering my kids, rebellious to my parents, then Satan is using me. I could be a pastor of a great congregation but if I don't waiteth, who's using me? I could have a word for everybody else but not for myself, who's using me? I'm talking in tongues for everybody else and can't talk tongues to myself, who's using me?

This message is for everybody. If ever I were to think church ain't it, I quickly realize who put that thought in my mind. I could think, you ain't ever going to be like them, they know more about the Bible than you. You ain't going to do this and you ain't going to do that because my style is unacceptable. You don't act like them. You don't dress like them. You don't talk like them. Your message ain't like theirs. You're talking about getting that rap out of church and no R&B mixing with the gospel and you're talking about no Christian compromising. Nobody wants to hear that. You're talking about posterity instead of prosperity. Nobody wants to hear that. People want to hear how they're going to get money.

Hell and destruction are never full. You have a choice today. Either you will keep letting Satan use you or start to let God use you. Hell is never full.